# Ray Dalio

*A Biography of the Legendary Investor*

By
Stephen Anderson

**© Copyright 2019 - All rights reserved.**

The content contained within this book may not be reproduced, duplicated or transmitted without direct written permission from the author or the publisher.

Under no circumstances will any blame or legal responsibility be held against the publisher, or author, for any damages, reparation, or monetary loss due to the information contained within this book, either directly or indirectly.

Legal Notice:

This book is copyright protected. It is only for personal use. You cannot amend, distribute, sell, use, quote or paraphrase any part, or the content within this book, without the consent of the author or publisher.

Disclaimer Notice:

Please note the information contained within this document is for educational and entertainment purposes only. All effort has been executed to present accurate, up to date, reliable, complete information. No warranties of any kind are declared or implied. Readers acknowledge that the author is not engaging in the rendering of legal, financial, medical or professional advice. The content within this book has been derived from various sources. Please consult a licensed professional before attempting any techniques outlined in this book.

By reading this document, the reader agrees that under no circumstances is the author responsible for any losses, direct or indirect, that are incurred as a result of the use of information contained within this document, including, but not limited to, errors, omissions, or inaccuracies.

# Table of Contents

Introduction ....................................................................... 6

Chapter 1: Stage of Life: Birth of an Investor (1949-1975) ............................................................................. 10

Chapter 2: Earliest Lessons ............................................ 28

Chapter 3: Stage of Life: Starting Bridgewater (1975-1982) ............................................................................. 32

Chapter 4: Learning from Failure .................................. 52

Chapter 5: Stage of Life: Road to Recovery (1982-1988) ............................................................................. 56

Chapter 6: Lessons from Recovery ................................ 67

Chapter 7: Stage of Life: Achieving Liftoff (1988-1995) ........................................................................ 71

Chapter 8: Lessons from Liftoff ..................................... 84

Chapter 9: Stage of Life: Coming to the Crossroads (1995- 2003) ..................................................................... 86

Chapter 10: Lessons from Crossroads ........................... 89

Chapter 11: Rapid Growth (2003-2006) ....................... 92

Chapter 12: Lessons from Rapid Growth ..................... 96

Chapter 13: Stage of Life: Psychological Revelations (2006-2008) .................................................................... 99

Chapter 14: Lessons from Psychology ......................... 104

Chapter 15: Stage of Life: Financial Crisis (2008-2010) ............................................................... 107

Chapter 16: Lessons from Crisis .................................... 115

Chapter 17: Going Public/Publishing Principles (2010-2011) ..................................................................... 118

Chapter 18: Lessons from Going Public ...................... 122

Chapter 19: European Debt Crisis (2010-2016) .......... 124

Chapter 20: Lessons from European Crisis ................. 131

Chapter 21: Stage of Life: An End and a Beginning (2016-2017) .................................................................... 136

Chapter 22: Lessons from End and Beginning ............ 140

Chapter 23: Stage of Life: Third Act (2017-Now) ........ 146

Chapter 24: Lessons from Third Act ............................ 156

Conclusion ..................................................................... 162

References ...................................................................... 167

# Introduction

What does it take to receive the title of the world's 58th wealthiest person of 2019?

Courage, smarts, and a hunger to be more. To do more. A desire to not accept circumstances as they are. The idea that if the grass is greener on the other side, then the only way to get there is through hard work and sheer determination. And, of course, a sense of ambition from a young age.

Many people might think that luck plays an important role in reaching a certain position, and that those who spend their time watching gorgeous sunsets on a million-dollar yacht somewhere in exotic waters overlooking lush beaches got there by winging it, and Lady Luck gave her blessings.

There is no denying it. Luck is an important factor when it comes to gaining or losing something in our lives. But distilling everyone's life into a matter of whether they had good or bad fortune is tantamount to ignoring their life's struggles. What had they faced before they reached a certain point in their lives? What challenges did they overcome? What defeats did they have to endure and keep pushing past despite the odds?

We improve our luck through our actions, and while that might sound like something that someone who hasn't experienced bad luck would say, it is still the truth. You improve your luck based on the actions you take. The more actions you perform, the more luck you create.

Take, for example, the idea of investing in a company at the age of 12.

A simple choice such as that is enough to create an opportunity and an avenue for success. The individual's luck improves as another branch opens in life filled with its own set of potentials.

At this point one might ask, "Who is this person who decided to invest at the age of 12? Who would have thought about it when all they should have been thinking about was their school, friends, sports, and maybe some fun and games? Just how much did the preteen invest and what changed?"

Before we go into that, it is important to know about the state of the world at that time. There were changes and events that would impact not just a few nations, but the entire world. We were exiting the after-effects of World War II, trying to rebuild countries and political and economic situations. But no one received an opportunity to take a breath, or if they did, it was a rather small breath. That's because shortly following the climax of the Second

World War, the Cold War immediately revealed its ugly side. Two powerful nations were locked in a state of impending nuclear threat, like two rams locking horns and waiting for one to give up. Racial tensions were reaching a feverish pitch with violence breaking out all across the United States and Civil Rights movements having a broader appeal. But it was also the time of the Space Age. The Soviet Union became the first nation to launch a person into space. With so much happening in the world and at home, it was unusual for a preteen to think about spending money as capital in a company. That does not mean that investment was an impossible thought. Rather, that thought would probably not be the first to enter the mind of someone who hadn't even finished high school and pondered their course in life.

But that did happen. Someone did have that thought and came to a certain conclusion that would change the course of that individual's history.

With that change came other milestones scattered throughout the person's life. Changes that were significant and remarkable. Choices and decisions that would bring the person into the Bloomberg's list of the wealthiest people of 2019.

While the destination itself sounds fantastic and definitely noteworthy, it is equally important to look at the journey. And that's what we are going to look at. The journey that led someone from a point where success was not the main focus, to a point where success became a definition.

But wait. Before we dive into the journey of the person, there is just one important thing left to do. An introduction.

I welcome you to take a glimpse into the life of Ray Dalio, now a billionaire hedge fund manager, investor, and philanthropist. We are going to look at his life before he acquired the billionaire status, the journey that led him to where he is now, and the lessons we can learn from a man who has lived a life that could easily be the plot of a Hollywood movie.

# Chapter 1: Stage of Life: Birth of an Investor (1949-1975)

August 8. Much of the first half of the 1940s was taken over by events surrounding World War II. You can pick any "August 8" from 1940 to 1945, and chances are there were probably more tragedies and conflicts recorded in history on those days than any hopeful or joyful events.

August 8, 1942. A group of German saboteurs had entered Washington to wreak havoc on the city's civil infrastructure. Thankfully, they were caught before they could bring any of their plans to fruition.

August 8, 1945. The Soviet Union decided to declare war on Japan. To show how serious they were about their decision, they readied over one million soldiers to enter Manchuria, which was a Japanese-occupied territory in China.

Looking at all of these events, it might seem that the date August 8 is one filled with chaos, war, and misery. Before 1945, any date would line up with some conflict, bloodshed, and strife. There was a reason it was called World War II; it affected all corners of the globe.

But what about the August 8s that followed the end of the World War in 1945? Surely they must have shown some remarkable, hopeful, and transformational events. That's not true at all. Post-1945 would bring about a few changes to the world, but most of the nations would be focused on repairs and reconstruction. Immigration would become a problem as people shifted away from war-torn countries and moved to places where there would be more opportunities.

And so it was the case with New York. Not only was the city becoming a home to European immigrants (because of which the Immigration Act of 1924 was enacted to stop the flow of immigrants into the country) because of the war, but add to that the problems of the Great Depression that took place from 1929 to 1939. New York (and for that matter, much of the United States) was in an economic recovery period.

And so, August 8, 1949, was not a date that promised a lot. Immigrants were still moving into New York from the after-effects of the war (this time, from many of the Asian countries). The economy was slowly but steadily trying to rebound.

It was this New York that Ray Dalio was born into. Because of that, Ray was not born into a family that could provide him with many opportunities. His father was a jazz musician. During the 1940s, the Jazz Age had created a big impression. The new music form was largely credited to African-Americans. But, eventually, one could notice a shift in the scene as the music became popular among white, middle-class citizens.

Back in the day, with racial tensions still high in many parts of America, accepting a form of art created by African-Americans was indeed a major cultural shift. This was because it gave an opportunity for many young people to challenge long-established traditions of previous generations. Of course, white jazz players would receive more recognition and opportunities to play on the radio. This was a huge communication medium back in the day. (Think of radio like the Netflix of the 20s, 30s, and 40s). But that would not stop the African-American jazz players from making the most out of every opportunity they received. As jazz grew in popularity, there were legends such as Louis Armstrong and Ella Fitzgerald making their mark in the jazz industry.

Eventually, jazz began to permeate into the white culture. It wasn't instant, but it grew into a form of music and an area that attracted many people. Subsequently, it blew up in the 1940s. People from all walks of life wanted to become part of this cultural phenomenon. After all, if African-Americans who had so few opportunities could go on to become legends, then surely others could follow in their footsteps. Many people wanted to be the next Miles Davis, John Coltrane, or Billie Holiday.

This is something that drew Ray's father, Marino Dallolio, into the world of jazz. There were opportunities, and he wanted to make use of those opportunities. Of course, just because someone thinks there is a chance they could make it big somewhere does not mean that they will. And this would be the case for Ray's father. Despite Dallolio's best efforts, he wouldn't be entering into the Hall of Fame or releasing his own records.

However, he did play the saxophone and clarinet in numerous jazz clubs around Manhattan, including the Copacabana. Today, the name Copacabana wouldn't even raise an eyebrow among many people. To them, it's just a club that has been lost to history. However, back in those days, the club was an icon. After all, it was featured in popular movies like Raging Bull, Carlito's Way, Goodfellas, French Connection, and Tootsie. Dallolio did have a bit of a reputation there.

Ray's mother, Ann, on the other hand, was a homemaker, which was part of the traditional role taken by women during those times.

There is a noticeable difference in the spelling of Ray's surname and his parents'; however, no reference could be located as to why Ray changed the spelling of his last name.

Growing up, Ray discovered something about himself; he wasn't great at remembering things. In fact, he would find it difficult to even recollect important facts, including phone numbers and dates. He would also discover another aspect about himself.

He didn't like following instructions.

You couldn't call him a rebel. That's because rebels are people who rise against authority. Ray never had problems with authority. But he was never one to easily follow the instructions that were given to him. Rather, he enjoyed figuring things out for himself. He was curious about the world around him and enjoyed the liberating feeling that discovering brought him.

He would also find school an ordeal that he had to go through. And it wasn't just because of the fact that there was too much information for him to remember.

At this point, I believe it is important to lay down some important aspects about Dalio's attention. It wasn't that he had a poor memory. On the contrary, he could remember things fairly well. He didn't find most information useful to him. It was not just the idea of simply memorizing facts and figures that meant little to him and convinced him that school was not what he wanted, but also that he didn't find the subjects taught by his teachers interesting. Whether it was arithmetic or language, they held little interest to him.

But his mother adored him, and he loved her equally. That would probably be the only reason why he would go through school. She would worry about his poor grades and sit with him through a lot of his lessons. He would show attention around her but couldn't sit through his lessons on his own.

It wasn't until age 12 that Dalio would find his calling.

He began to work as a caddy at a reputed golf course. And, no, being a caddy wasn't his life's calling. He only worked at that job so that he could start contributing toward his family's income. It was a way to make ends meet and help his father with some of the work.

It was around that time that word about investing in the stock market started floating around. Back then, people said the growth of the U.S. economy, and the dollar in particular, resulted in opportunities for many, but only few knew what to do with them.

Ray Dalio knew exactly what he would do with his money. To accomplish his goal, he saved up some of what he earned as a caddy and borrowed a small amount from his father. He wanted to play the stock market, so he bought $300 worth of shares from Northeast Airlines. Back then, he didn't have an idea of how the stock market worked. He thought that the more shares he had in his hands, the more money he could make. It was a dumb strategy, but it worked through sheer luck. Northeast Airlines was bought by another company, and Dalio's money tripled. The taste of success was invigorating. Sure, Dalio hadn't planned any strategy, but he could see the potential. And so, he decided to learn.

Back then, Fortune magazine would feature tear-out coupons that one could mail to the company and receive annual reports from Fortune 500 companies. Ray did not pick out coupons for just one or two companies—he ordered them all.

In fact, it reached a point where the mailman had to lug all the reports to his door, and he wore an expression that showed that he would rather be anywhere but at the Dallalio's doorstep. He was also perplexed that the recipient of those records was a 13-year-old boy.

Ray began to pore through those records, absorbing all the details he could find. As he was going through the records, he also kept a close eye on the stock market, which was slowly rising.

Eventually, he took a serious interest in the markets. He started playing the market and taking risks. Ray loved risks. Even when it concerned situations outside of the market, he would enjoy the thrill of doing something not many people would do. One of those risky activities involved faking IDs so that he could take his friends to concerts, music festivals, bars, and wherever else they wouldn't be allowed to enter. The results from those risks made taking them even more fulfilling. And when things didn't work out? Well, he moved on to the next one.

Ray's fear was not getting caught or losing at something. His fear was mediocrity and boredom. He did not like the mundane and the ordinary. He wanted to take what opportunities he had and risk them for a bigger reward.

And that worked out well for him.

The year was 1966. The stock market was booming. Between February of 1956 and February of 1966, the market had more than doubled. There was a gain of over 111%, something that was unheard of since the 1920s. Whoever took risks in the market saw a huge return. Ray was making money. He was on top of the world. Of course, his money would go into surfing or enjoying all of the things that high-schoolers would be involved in.

But what goes up has to come down at some point. And Ray would discover that the boom in the market is not a permanent fixture. That was when he got the true picture of what the market is capable of.

In the year 1966, there was widespread optimism among the investors. They were looking at a future that would rake in millions, maybe billions, for some. But from 1967 onward, there would be some economic surprises that would send price declines throughout the market.

That year, Ray was taught his first lesson; even though people place high expectations for the stock market, the reality was much different. He kept buying shares, spending money, and putting blind faith in the ideas of other investors who were expecting the market to rebound. It had happened before. Surely there would be no reason for it to not happen again, right? Sadly, the bull market (the name given to a market that shows a rise) that ended in 1966 would not gain the same level of rise until 1980, more than 14 years later.

Ray stopped buying shares. He realized something. The market prices were dependent on people's expectations. They increased if the prices were better than what people expected and dropped when the prices were worse than expected.

Despite the harsh lesson learned, Ray would not be deterred. In fact, he went back to learning more about the market. He would soon be entering college. This meant that he could pick subjects that interested him and not be forced to go through lessons that meant nothing to him, which was what he faced in high school. This choice of picking the subjects that interested him would soon be reflected in Ray's grades.

He would go from averaging Cs to getting straights As. His mother was definitely proud. But, sadly, she would not be for long.

She would pass away when Dalio was 19.

The event would be a hard blow for the teenager. He would often wonder if he would ever find a reason to smile again. She was a rock in his life and was his main source of support.

With all that was happening in his life, Ray would find it overwhelming to deal with anything. Things were not looking good for him. He was faced with a personal and financial loss, the former devastating and the latter less so. Regardless, his mother's death took a toll on him.

He wanted to have some peace to think clearly.

Back then, the Beatles' music was everywhere. In 1968, the British band made news when they visited India and spoke at length about Transcendental Meditation. In fact, the 1960s was the time of the hippie culture, and it would have a great influence in the West. It was this culture that saw hundreds of thousands of people travel to India to learn more about a transformative form of meditation—

yoga. The hippie culture and the Beatles played a significant role in spreading yoga to different parts of the West. People were fascinated with the idea of yoga. They wanted to learn more. They wanted to practice it.

Ray wanted to practice it as well.

And it would benefit Ray greatly. After his recent losses, mediation would bring a sense of open-mindedness that would encourage him to think with more clarity. The cobwebs in his mind would slowly disappear, allowing him to plan for his future.

That was when he decided to attend college and major in finance. Ray loved the markets, and he knew that he would get a wealth of additional information that he could use to his benefit. His choice would help in more ways than one. After joining his preferred class, he was introduced to the world of commodities. Surprisingly, the person who introduced him to commodities happened to be a Vietnam veteran who was a bit older than Ray. Life does have its twists and turns.

Meditation, finance, and college would have a unique effect on Ray. He entered the realm of drug experimentation that was capable of expanding minds, free-love, and the rejecting traditional authority. Yes, while Ray had never had problems with authority, he began to display a slight tendency to rebel against authoritative figures.

He would also be deeply inspired by Steve Jobs, who had also taken up meditation and refused to learn traditional subjects. Jobs preferred to build and visualize things.

At that time, Ray's father would be a big influence in his life. If you are thinking that this story is going to go in the direction of an alcoholic or abusive father and a child who grew up wanting to leave home, you are sorely mistaken. Ray's father loved his son. He would often work late into the night until the earning hours of the morning. They never had the chance to spend a lot of time together. His father would often encourage Ray to take up responsibilities, but the newly-developed rebelliousness nature would often get in the way of doing anything. Still, Ray would never openly reject his father. It was not out of fear, but out of love and respect for a man who did everything possible to make sure that his son grew up with a certain set of principles. For the most part, Ray's father would stay away from any direct influence on his life. But that would change in the years following 1969.

At the time, the Vietnam War was sending the country into a difficult phase. As more and more body bags returned to the United States, those who were opposed to the war increased. It almost seemed as though the entire country was split, with pro- and anti-Vietnam War supporters on either side. Eventually, a lottery-based system was established whereby people would be drafted into the war based on their birthdates. Ray would remember listening to the radio as the announcer read out the birth dates that would be drafted. Even though only 160 birthdays were going to be read on air, the announcer read all 366 dates on his list, one for each day of the year. Ray's birthday was the 48th one read during the announcement. At that time, Ray wasn't wise enough about the ways of the war to decide against it. He was of the opinion that nothing could happen to him.

His father had a different opinion. Even though Marino Dallolio was part of both World War II and the Korean War, he was hell-bent on preventing Ray from enlisting. Dallolio took his son to the doctor, who then discovered that Ray had hypoglycemia. While the condition was not as serious as other forms of diseases, it was still something that the army wouldn't accept. Hypoglycemia is a condition that is caused when the body has very low levels of blood sugar, or glucose. The condition is treatable, but one cannot have a soldier trying to medicate himself in the middle of the battlefield when bullets are zipping by and mortar fire is powerful enough to excavate the earth. Ray was given an exemption from participating in the war. Why an exemption? Because anyone whose birthday was read during the announcement had to enlist for the war.

Ray got out of being part of the war because of a technicality. He wasn't happy about it. But when he looked back to the moment years later, he could only appreciate his dad's love and the efforts he took to protect his son. In fact, Ray was unsure what he would have done if he had been drafted. His life would never have been the same, that's for sure. Goodbye hedge fund manager, and hello Post-Traumatic Stress Disorder, or PTSD.

It was around the year 1971 that there would be a major shift in the currency market. Until that point, most people around the world would never have thought to pay attention to currency rates. After all, currency had been stable for a long time. Before 1971, gold was the preferred method of currency exchange between countries, with the U.S. dollar serving as the price of gold. In 1971, the modern foreign exchange as we know it would be born, where nation's currencies would be valued based on the nation's economic and political situations. There would be no need for gold, but the U.S. would still be used for many of the exchange rates. This compelled Ray to look deeper into the currency market and learn more about it. At the same time, in the spring of 1971, he graduated college with a near-perfect grade point average.

He was accepted into Harvard Business School.

Before he could start at Harvard, he worked for a brief while at the New York Stock Exchange; his curiosity to learn more about currency taking him to the one place where it was dealt in huge amounts.

Ray would spend the entire summer trying to grasp as much as he could about "fluctuations" and "devaluations" and all the other important phrases that would make up the world of currency. When he finally began his journey at Harvard Business School, he was eager to meet the people there, those he thought he could gain some valuable insights and wisdom from.

And he was not left disappointed. In fact, he discovered something that exceeded his expectations.

There were no teachers who used a blackboard to explain the various topics. One had to study various case studies and then analyze them in detail. Students were grouped together, and they would have to come up with all the solutions that could be taken by the people in the situations presented in the case studies. To Ray, it was his kind of school!

In 1972, after reliance on gold was dropped and the dollar was once again the main currency in the market, the printing of new currency soared. The markets were showing a rise and the economy was improving considerably. Despite all of this, Ray was more interested in the commodities market, which was a surprise since most people–if not everyone–who graduated from Harvard Business School and wanted to trade preferred to enter into the stock market. Surprise was the same reaction that the director of Merrill Lynch had when Ray requested to work for him. Why commodities? Stock is the next best thing! Despite everything, the director allowed Ray to focus his attention on the commodities market. Perhaps Ray's enthusiasm and interest were infectious. Maybe he saw something in Ray's determination. Whatever it was, the director seemed to be impressed by it.

In 1973, the commodities market took a dive.

During this time, the U.S. was an open ally of Israel. While the alliance itself was frowned upon by many nations, no one had any reason to take action against it. Most of the resistance came in the form of proclamations and public speeches. Words were given much weight rather than actions.

That all changed during the Yom Kippur War.

It was October 6, a few days before the holiest day in Judaism. Israel was in a festive mood, unaware that a coalition had taken place between numerous Arab states led by Egypt. Their strategy? To use their military prowess to seize control of the Suez Canal and use that to negotiate the release of Sinai, which was under Israeli control during the time. Sinai itself was an important religious landmark, and numerous Arab nations felt that it was in the wrong hands.

What was initially supposed to be an Arab-Israel conflict took a turn for the worse when the U.S. decided to intervene to support its ally. The Arab nations, viewing the support as an act of betrayal, decided to take extreme measures. They had finally found their reason to act against the U.S.-Israel alliance.

In October 1973, members of the Organization of Arab Petroleum Exporting Countries, or OPEC for short, raised an oil embargo against all nations supporting Israel, including the U.S. The results were catastrophic. Oil prices soared from $3 a barrel to $12. That was a staggering 400% increase. The commodities market took a hit.

As a response, the Federal Reserve System tightened its monetary policy, which is essentially the reactions that central banks take when inflation is too strong.

Ray watched as the situation unfurled. His keen insights and his curiosity to learn more helped him understand the circumstances that led to the stock market's position.

It would be another lesson in the young man's learning journey.

In 1974, Ray was living in New York with one of his classmates from Harvard who was dating a Cuban woman. He set Ray up on a blind date with a Spanish woman named Barbara Ray, who he would come to describe as "exotic." The woman could barely speak English and the couple would have difficulty communicating, but that did not stop the duo from hitting it off.

Eventually, they would be married and would go on to have four sons.

At the same time, Bridgewater was born.

# Chapter 2: Earliest Lessons

One of the first things that Ray learned about himself was that he couldn't retain information that he did not perceive as important. This reality was something that he was able to become comfortable with.

In life, it is important to understand how reality works. There are things that people are capable of and there are things that they are not interested in. Being a Jack-of-all-trades has a nice ring to it and could definitely impress people. But that is not what will get you far in life. Ray always believed in dealing with reality. Rather than have an unnatural state of mind that tends to focus on make-believes and what-ifs, Ray understood that what was happening in the present is more important than what someone can expect from the future or the tragedies of the past. It is important to have a strong mental fortitude and use that to your advantage.

On the other hand, being emotional is a natural reaction. Ray discovered that when facing reality, he would face all kinds of emotions. Sometimes, they would lead to a good outcome and, sometimes, they would only cause more problems. But either way, Ray believed that the key to making the most out of life was to use logic. If the emotions aligned with logic, only then should people make a decision. That way, they would make thoughtful decisions. This was apparent throughout his early life, as he never thought to simply disagree with something because he would be frustrated or angry. To Ray, when he thought of things rationally, he realized that certain decisions or factors in his life did not add any value. For example, his grades suffered in school not because he despised the subjects being taught or any of the teachers. He wasn't depressed or disappointed. He simply did not find any value in it. When he was working as a caddy, his logic guided him toward the stock market because he was genuinely interested in playing the market.

When Ray entered college, he picked up finance as his subject of focus, not merely because he liked it, but because he knew it would benefit him greatly.

While many people thought that Ray's adventurous behavior meant that he was reckless, the reality of the situation was far from the assumption. You see, Ray focused on big goals. He believed that stretching his goals allowed him to take bigger risks and bigger rewards. But, more importantly, it puts him in a position to fail. Ray loved to fail because of the lessons he could learn from it. These lessons would guide him down a better path and encourage him to think innovatively. He understood that the faster he failed, the quicker he would learn, and the earlier he would be prepared to face the challenges in the future. He aimed to have the upper hand, but he knew that being in that position did not happen easily.

But Ray is no Terminator. He is not an emotionless android. He does feel the pain, disappointments, and blowbacks from his failures. He does not like the emotions that failures bring. But he keeps those feelings in perspective. He knows that he will get through those setbacks, and that most of his learnings will come by understanding them rather than reacting to them. Once again, his rational and pragmatic behavior takes over, dealing with the emotions and focusing on what's important; the lesson itself.

This rational perspective in life had allowed Ray to grow tremendously and quickly. After all, he was already playing the markets when he was in high school and making a profit from it. How many high schoolers can boast that? On that note, how many twelve-year-old's can claim to have successfully invested in the stock market?

Ray wasn't an irrational thrill-seeker. Yes, he did enjoy taking risks and the thrills that they would bring. But he was always pragmatic. If something failed, he would learn from it and try and do it better. Ray also understood the need for radical open-mindedness. He believed that learning is the result of a feedback loop that happens constantly. When you are open-minded to this learning process, then your actions become clear to you. You won't become a victim of misunderstanding. Take, for example, a decision that was made based on an emotional reaction. Think about that decision and ponder if was made in a clear state of mind or not. More often than not, you might find out that the reasons behind that emotional decision are rather vague.

Don't lose your sense of adventure. If you do not take chances, you won't discover incredible opportunities.

# Chapter 3: Stage of Life: Starting Bridgewater (1975-1982)

1975.

Starting a business is a whole new ballgame. One that is played on a court that has tough rules and tougher opponents. But that wouldn't stop Ray.

Always looking for opportunities, Ray had an idea of where he would go after he graduated from Harvard Business School. He had experience in commodities and held a Harvard MBA. That made him a hot commodity (no pun intended). He was eventually hired as Director of Commodities at Dominick & Dominick for $25,000 a year. The pay was among the top salaries of what Harvard Business School graduates could earn in that year. To Ray, it was not a bad deal. Besides, he couldn't deny the fact that "Director of Commodities" had a nice ring to it. His mission: to set up the commodities division. One thing that Ray realized was that he was in way over his head to deal with a task like that. Setting up an entire division takes years of experience. But Ray's arrogance got the better of him. Ever so adventurous and the risk-taker that he was, he ignored the very rules he had set up in life: to think things through.

The stock market in 1975 was still not recovered, and it affected the business of Dominick & Dominick. The company had no choice but to shut down its operations and file for bankruptcy. The move would have left Ray without a job and a tough loss to recover from. Thankfully, we have learned about his risk-taking nature by now, and we should have probably expected this; he had set up a small business with a friend from Harvard Business School, Bob Scott. Using Bob's and his Harvard friends' connections, the duo reached out to people from other countries. Their goal was to sell commodities from the U.S. Ray and Bob named their business Bridgewater, since the idea of reaching out to clients from other countries was "bridging the waters," according to the two owners. Toward the end of 1975, there wasn't much left of the business, but since it was already established on paper, Ray decided to keep it.

At that time, Ray was working out of his two-bedroom apartment. He was sharing the apartment with a friend from Harvard, who decided to move out. This gave Ray an empty room, and rather than invite someone else to live in with him, he decided to turn the apartment into an office. He began to work with another friend with whom he used to play rugby and even hired a young woman to work as an assistant.

And that was the entirety of Bridgewater. Just three people in a two-bedroom apartment. If you are wondering as to the mystery of Bob, he had decided to leave the company when it seemed that it was not gaining any initial success.

For the most part, Ray spent his time following the markets and placing himself into the positions of his corporate clients. His strategy was to show his clients that he was capable of handling and managing market risks. And he never stopped trading himself. He had a personal trading account, and he would use that to keep playing the market. The job did not provide much in the way of profits. But to Ray, the fact that he was helping his clients beat the markets and earning enough to make sure that basic needs were always met made him happy.

1977. Ray and Barbara had been living together for a while now. They were ready to take the next step forward in their relationship. They wanted to have a child. Before that, they had to take care of the minor situation of marriage, and in the same year, Ray and Barbara were newlyweds. They decided that if they were indeed going to have children, then doing so in their current two-bedroom apartment was not the way to go. And so the couple packed their bags and shifted to a brownstone in Manhattan, which would be a step up from their former standard of living. Ray even shifted his business into the brownstone. At the same time, there were many Russian businesses in New York that were into the grain business. Having heard of Ray's reputation, they decided to seek his advice on the grain market. For Ray and Barbara, that was an opportunity for a romantic getaway, so the couple headed to the USSR on a business-honeymoon. They landed in Moscow on New Year's Eve and their trip turned out to be more eventful than they had imagined. They ended up partying with many fun-loving Russians, and the trip itself showed Ray the joys of travel.

He decided that his business could be a way for him to travel to exotic places while making money at the same time. It was definitely a double-win situation.

The Russians had opened new doors of opportunity for Ray. He became involved in grain, meat, livestock, and oilseed markets. He enjoyed working with them because they were less influenced by perceptions of value than stocks. You see, the stock could hit new highs and new lows based on people buying or selling them, which was eventually based on how those very same people viewed the markets. But products like livestock ended up in the meat market and would be priced based on the purchasing ability of the consumer. Ray was able to map the various processes that brought the livestock from the farm to the customer. He was able to understand the relationships between the processes and the factors that guided those relationships. Since most livestock consume grain (which would mostly consist of corn) along with soymeal, and since the soymeal and corn usually vie for acreage, those markets would not be so much different from each other. Ray began to delve into those markets and understand as much as he could about them–the typical yields and the acreage required for planting in the important growing areas; understanding the rainfall levels so that they could, in turn, be used to determine yield estimates; projecting carrying costs, harvest sizes, and inventories of the livestock based on location, group, and rates of weight gain; the amount of livestock to be slaughtered each season; and many other factors.

It wasn't complicated. It wasn't rocket science. Ray could easily break down information and arrange it in meaningful ways. He had done it before (only when he was interested, of course), and he could do it now. But he wasn't naive to think that he could learn everything on his own. And so he asked for help from the people who were in the agriculture and livestock business for a long time. Mostly, he wanted them to teach him everything they knew about growing crops necessary for livestock. Whatever Ray learned, he arranged them into models and understood not only the obvious connections, but those that would take people a little while to see.

Here's an example. When Ray examined the number of hogs, chickens, and cattle that were being fed at one time, the amount of grain they were given, and the rate at which they grew, he could easily identify how much meat would arrive in the market and when that meat would be available. Ray was also able to measure how much soybeans and corn were required, how much soybeans and corn he could acquire based on rainfall conditions and based on the weather factors, and the quality of the grain he would receive.

Ray loved the entire process of measuring and predicting outcomes. It was as though he was watching different parts of a machine all working together to achieve a particular result. Looking at the interconnectedness of everything, he could make decisions or rules. Ray was good at it and loved everything about it. He could also create models based on everything he learned.

However, the models he used were much different from the advanced ones found today. The technology back in those days could only do so much, unlike the complex simulations, calculations, and projections that can be performed by current computer technology. But despite the technology back then, Ray loved building models and making decisions based on their output. While they were not advanced, they were enough to bring him good profits. He would also use all the knowledge that he gained about demand and supply from his studies at Harvard Business School. However, what he learned from his classes at Harvard was that both demand and supply were measured in terms of how much was sold. He changed his viewpoint. He began to measure demand in terms of the amount spent (instead of the quantity sold), who the buyers and the sellers in the market were, and the reasons for their purchase and sale.

By changing his mindset, Ray was able to look at the market from a different perspective. He was able to catch on to important market and economic shifts before others could. Whenever Ray examined any market–whether it was commodities, stocks, currencies, bonds, or any other instrument–he could easily recognize and understand imbalances that people who used the traditional form of demand and supply definitions would not be able to detect.

While Ray was able to understand the market from a unique perspective, it did not mean that his method was perfect. On the contrary, he would learn some valuable lessons. He would remember the time he had made a bet of $100,000 on a hunch that he could not lose, based on projections made from his method of thinking. He lost. At that time, that money was his net worth. But what affected him more than the loss of the money was the loss it had on his clients. Ray learned a valuable lesson that he had previously understood but had forgotten along the way: you can never be sure of anything. From that point onward, he would never forget the lesson. In fact, he changed his mindset. He realized that no matter what happened, there would always be risks. It was better to assume that things could go wrong, even when you are certain they won't. It was always best to assume that you were missing something, rather than assuming that you have covered every avenue.

Expect the best. Prepare for the worst.

At the same time, Ray would realize something even more important about life. He would realize that it was not always about the what, but about the who as well. He recognized that while it was always good to make more money, it was far better to have wonderful people and meaningful relationships in life.

One of the beliefs he began to nurture within himself was the idea that money itself has no intrinsic value. We give it value based on what it is capable of purchasing. After all, what a dollar can get you might not be the same thing that a yen is capable of purchasing.

The most important fact about money is that it couldn't buy everything. Ray understood that. His idea was to put weight on things in life. It was as though he was trying to gauge the value of various life components. He discovered that he put equal value on making money and maintaining his relationships. He would never cross the line where he would have to sacrifice his relationships to make more money. In fact, there was no amount of money that would convince him to give up on the people he loved.

Which is why, during the late 1970s, he wasn't thinking of making a million dollars through his business. He was enjoying the work he had and the people in his life. Rather, he wanted to act in an advisory position. He began to send the various observations that he made about the market to his clients. Over time, the number of requests increased when it eventually reached a point where he was sending the same advice to different clients. At that point, Ray was hit with an idea: what if he could compile all his learnings, information, and advice into one medium? That led to the birth of *Daily Observations*, a publication that provided the latest information about the markets. Today, after 40 years and with over 10,000 editions published, *Daily Observations* has become one of the go-to materials for policymakers, clients, and businesses around the world.

But the late 70s were also a time of great market changes. You see, ever since the dollar was delinked from gold in 1971, there were three giant waves of debt and inflation. The first one occurred in 1971. The dollar became devalued and the United States Congress had to release a statement claiming that the reason for the devaluation was to ensure that they were protecting the dollar. The second waves of debt and inflation fluctuations happened between 1974 and 1975, and it took the level of inflation to its highest level since the conclusion of World War II. Interest rates soared through the roof, reaching a peak that was unseen since the 1930s. But the final wave was going to hit the hardest. When it happened from 1979-1982, inflation and interest rates went up and down with such frequency that commodities, currencies, stocks, and bonds all went through an intense period of volatility. No one could predict anything and the economy suffered because of it. In fact, the unemployment rates were so high that they hadn't been this bad since the Great Depression. All of these situations gave Ray the opportunity to become wiser about the market. It would even help him predict the market.

The market was never based on a single component. It was a mix of various factors that could send it to new heights or the deepest of lows. Ray understood that all of these factors could come together to decide the future of the market. He immersed himself into understanding it even more. After all, one cannot stop the learning process.

At the same time, Bridgewater was growing into a success. During his dealings with the beef and cattle industry, he had come into contact with Paul Colman, who would go on to become Ray's good friend and eventually join Bridgewater. Paul was someone whose intellect and values were something that Ray respected. After Ray managed to convince him that they would do things to conquer the world together, Paul brought his wife and kids from Oklahoma to Manhattan. The two families would eventually become inseparable. Things seemed too good to be true. Not only did Ray have a good friend to work with, but he loved the fact that his family had discovered strong connections with another family.

In 1981, the two partners decided that they would like to raise their families in a country setting, away from the hustle and bustle of the city life. And so, the two families, along with Bridgewater and all its staff, shifted to Connecticut. The work became even more rewarding. Ray and Paul would bounce ideas, theories, and market forces and situations between them. This would enable both men to gain a deeper understanding of market situations. They would often plug in data and calculations into their computer at the end of the day and would check to see the results the next morning. Ray was all about experimenting and learning. This was reflected in the way both men approached their work.

Which brings us back to the third wave of market fluctuations. Because Ray was able to learn more with Paul, he understood the direction the market was going to take. The volatility of the market was at an all-time high. The Federal Reserve System, or Fed for short, had only two options.

1) They could start printing more money to relieve the debt problems that they were facing. But this would mean pushing the inflation rate even higher, which was already pushing 10%. Why does printing money increase inflation? That's because the more money a country prints, the more worthless it becomes. Remember that the currency also moves in the Foreign Exchange market. If people start noticing the sudden influx of currency in the economy, they are all going to start panicking. Their only option is to bet against the currency, and that does not bode well for any country.

2) On the other hand, the Fed could tighten the economy. Essentially, what this means is that they raise the interest rates of the currency. This would prevent a large influx of foreign

investments and spending, but it would keep the economy from growing too fast. Now most people might think that a fast-growing economy is a positive sign. So isn't an incredibly fast-growing economy good for the country? Not quite. You see, a country only has a finite amount of capital and labor. Using those two factors, it can estimate just how much growth it can handle at any point in time. Imagine if the growth happens way beyond the country's control or ability to manage. The inflation rates would shoot through the roof.

The U.S. was showing signs of a deteriorating economy. Inflation was increasing and the economic activity was worsening; two of the worst combinations of events to occur in a country. Since Ray was already studying the market, he published a column in the *Daily Observations* that was titled, "The Next Depression in Perspective."

Ray's viewpoints were extremely controversial. That is because people do not like to think of something terrible happening to them. They believe that the word "depression" is simply a scare tactic used by economists and news outlets, not something a rational thinking person would ever choose to employ. But Ray had been studying the market closely through all the fluctuations that had occurred and even all the way back to the 1800s.

He had also done his share of calculations and knew there was a crisis of debt just waiting to happen. He shared his studies with his clients. Because of the controversial nature of his viewpoints, he had asked others to refute his discoveries. He encouraged them to find flaws in his reasoning. No one could find any. Yet, no one was willing to endorse his discovery.

Ray believed that eventually, it would come down to two options. Either there would be a deflationary depression or accelerating inflation, which was why he was holding on to both bonds (which perform well in a deflationary depression) and gold (which does well in situations of accelerating inflation). Ray felt that holding such instruments was much better than investing in stocks or currencies.

When the results of the market came in, they were against Ray.

Turns out, his predictions were wrong at that time. It seemed that Ray's viewpoints would be considered a scare tactic after all. One thing that Ray had understood when he was dealing with his previous trades was that everything depended on timing. He was so sure about the fact that the market would eventually turn.

In the end, he wasn't right.

He was spot on.

The markets did turn. The policies enacted by the Feds began to take a devastating turn. Ray's investments started showing returns, just like he predicted they would. His supposed "scare tactics" turned out to be real. Anyone who had doubted Ray at that time would find no reason to doubt him anymore.

August 1982. Mexico had defaulted on its debts. Economic repercussions were being felt throughout the world. At that time, people knew that if one country would not be able to make payments on its loans, other countries would soon follow. This was a big problem because the U.S. had allowed for nearly 250% of its capital to be taken by other countries as loans. Any activity related to business loans came to a complete stop, as though someone had flipped a switch.

Ray and a few others had predicted all of this, and for that reason, he found himself gaining attention. Eventually, Congress began to hold hearings on the economic crisis and the state of the country's debts. Ray was invited to testify and bring in his expertise on the matter. This garnered even more attention and, eventually, he was invited to appear on a popular show, *Wall $treet Week with Louis Rukeyser*. With the power of his research and his confidence, he declared that the country was headed toward a depression. In other words, the economy would fail. He provided theories and explanations, detailing all the reasons he had discovered.

At that time, the Fed had to provide a response to the massive defaults that the other countries were going through. They started releasing more money into the economy. The move came as a bit of a surprise to Ray, but he thought of it as a knee-jerk reaction to the economic situation. Often, when people witness something extreme happen in an economy, they end up taking sudden reactions to react or recover from it. The reactions are taken to avoid too much loss or start taking in as much profits as possible. Ray estimated that there was a 75% chance that despite the Fed's best efforts, the economy would head into a downward spiral. There was a 20% chance that there would indeed be a recovery, but it wouldn't last long and the economy would still fail. The remaining five percent was hedged on the fact that after the economy would recover temporarily, it would enter hyperinflation, which is also a terrible situation for the economy to be in. This time, Ray was going to prepare for the worst. He began to put his bets on T-bills (short for Treasury bills) and gold, which was what people invested in when they knew that a country's credit problems would eventually increase.

In the end, he wasn't right.

And this time, he was dead wrong.

After a brief delay, the efforts of the Fed began to pay off. The economy rebounded without any inflation, let alone hyperinflation. The stock market began to slowly move into a bull situation, showing improvements year after year. In fact, over the next 18 years, the U.S. economy would enjoy incredible non-inflationary growth, one of the greatest in its economic history.

But what happened? Ray was certain about the direction of the market. There was no way he could have been wrong with the information he had. In the end, he figured it out himself. His earlier predictions were based on the fact that many other countries would follow Mexico. They would default on their loans. However, what really happened was that money began pouring into the U.S. economy from the countries that had borrowed money. That way, the dollar price went up and the Fed was able to avoid inflation as it slowly began to lower interest rates.

How did the countries manage to pay back what they owed?

The International Monetary Fund (IMF), a global monetary organization that comprises 189 member countries, was able to help the borrowers of the U.S. dollar settle their debts through new loan schemes. That would allow the countries to pay back their loans using a different financial scheme, one that was much easier on them.

Ray's mistake would cost him everything. The huge loss was like being punched in the stomach; no one saw it coming and the blow was damaging. Not only was Ray wrong, he was publicly proven to be wrong. Everything he had declared on public television amounted to nothing. After eight years, all he could do was watch his business crumbling around him.

And while all of this occurred, Ray's responsibilities had doubled.

You see, his first son, Devon, was born in 1978, and his second son, Paul, was born in 1979.

He had lost the business while having a family to take care of.

Ray lost so much money that he was unable to pay the people who worked with him and under him. With a heavy heart, he had to let them go one by one. Eventually, it came down to just two employees; him and his best friend, Paul Colman.

Eventually, Colman wanted to leave as well.

The departure was not easy. Both families had plenty of tears to show for it. But the decision had been made, and

Colman and his family moved back to Oklahoma. Bridgewater became a shell of its previous self, a lonely place filled with just one employee: Ray.

It was difficult for Ray to lose not just the people he cared about deeply, but the business that he had put so much effort into. The decline was devastating. Ray could not find the means to make ends meet and had to take $4,000 from his father until he could find a way to sell his car.

He had a choice. Should he become an employee again? That was not what he wanted in life because that would mean closing down a business he had built from the ground up, admitting defeat, and going in a backward direction from a business owner to an employee. Leaving that option meant continuing with his business, which could not provide him the means to take care of his family. He had two sons to think about, and he was on the precipice of a tough decision. Whatever he chose to do would not only impact his life, but his family's future.

Before the business's crash, Ray was also buying and selling in the markets on his clients' behalf. Sometimes, he would earn a fixed fee from the clients, and at other times, he would get a share of the profits. The payment scheme was never fixed. As the number of clients grew, he began to manage buying and selling for Lane Processing, which was the largest chicken producer at that time, and McDonald's, which was a huge buyer of beef. With Ray's insights, Lane Processing eventually began to make more money from the soy and grain markets than it did from selling its chickens, which was no easy feat to accomplish.

It was during that time that Ray was presented with another problem. McDonald's wanted to introduce Chicken McNuggets into the market. The product was rather innovative at that time. But they were hesitant about introducing it because they were worried about the fact that, after seeing the new product (which they were certain would succeed), the chicken prices would increase and their profit margins would diminish, which meant coming to an agreement with Lane Processing where the price of chicken would be fixed. However, Lane Processing would not agree to the conditions because they were concerned that when the cost of raising chickens would eventually increase and they still kept their costs the same, then their profit margins would suffer.

Ray came up with a solution. He explained to Lane Processing how they could combine soy and corn to arrive at a cost that would benefit them greatly. McDonald's agreed and the two companies entered an agreement in 1983. Sadly, they did so without Ray's company, as Bridgewater was near collapse.

# Chapter 4: Learning from Failure

Ray had failed. He had made decisions based on his arrogance.

But he was a learner and that would be the biggest takeaway from his many failures. He believed that the act of learning never stopped. One never stopped taking risks because they were afraid of failure. In fact, as he discovered, there were risks in everything, even in seemingly safe choices and bets.

At the same time, Ray believed that failures should teach us the value of being cautious. No matter how sure we think we are about something, it is better to imagine that we haven't covered everything and take the prudent course of action by evaluating every step we have taken towards our decision.

Failure itself is a rather gut-wrenching situation. It can deplete us of our emotional, mental, and physical reserves. Many people experience failure to eventually become paralyzed by it. But Ray had a different approach to failure. His idea was to gain whatever lessons he could from it so that he could go back and remake the decision, but this time using an entirely new set of ideas and tactics.

One could always argue that Ray hadn't felt enough failures. Sometimes, it is not about the lessons you learn because no matter how hard you try, you end up failing. Despite the careful assessment of the scenario and avoiding the mistakes of the past, failure becomes inevitable. It does not take one failure to bring success. What many don't realize is that Ray never bounced back from just one failure. He himself admitted that it was only through many mistakes and failures that he would eventually change his approach.

Which brings us to another important reaction to failure. Never give up after just one incident. Ray realized this a long time ago. When he learned from his failures, he would apply his newfound teachings to discover new ideas and paths. If he failed again, then he knew that his lesson was never complete. That's what set him apart from others. Even if he was confident about something, he learned to expect failure as something that could always occur. This meant that his lessons were never over. There would always be something to learn and he was always ready to absorb the lessons.

Of course, you could see that Ray had eventually understood how his arrogance cost him everything. He realized that if he ever was going to come back from all his losses again, he would have to find a way to deal with the natural aggressiveness that he had.

Ray had also come to an obvious conclusion. Even after everything that had happened, he would still continue to go after the life that he had built, with all its risks and pitfalls. This time, however, he would have to find ways to cross the complexities of life without ending up in another pitfall. And that is another valuable lesson to understand. When you have found your calling, nothing should distract you from its path. Things are never going to be easy. There are going to be events that are going to question your decision and focus. But only you can decide if you are willing to learn from them and push through, aiming for the goal that you set for yourself, or give up and let go of everything you believe in.

Understand this: it doesn't matter how slowly you go. What matters is that you do not stop. Ray understood this after his big fall. He knew that his brash and arrogant behavior—where he would not take things slow—led to his downfall.

Furthermore, learning only stops when you want it to stop. No matter how much you think you know about a subject, there is always more knowledge to gain. Never put your arrogance on the line where you convince yourself that you know everything there is to know about something.

Be a student. Learn. Practice. Fail. Learn again. Practice again. Maybe fail again. Repeat as many times as necessary.

Finally, succeed.

# Chapter 5: Stage of Life: Road to Recovery (1982-1988)

1983.

Ray was so broke that he couldn't afford to meet his clients. This was a problem for the reason that one of his prospective clients was in Texas, and Ray was unable to save up enough money to buy the plane ticket to head there. Although Ray knew that the fees he would earn from the client would cover the fare of the ticket many times over, he would still refuse to fly all the way there. He just couldn't.

Despite the setbacks, Ray was slowly bringing back his business. He started adding more clients, team members, and, of course, revenue. The growth wasn't substantial, but to Ray, it was a positive direction for his company. In fact, he would only focus on the work. He would never think of his endeavors as a way to rebuild the company.

Computers would play an important role in the growth of the business. Back then, many businesses did not require a computer, but to Ray they were an invaluable asset to the company. Many of the projections and calculations were possible because of computers.

In 1946, the world's first computer was introduced to the world. Named ENIAC (which was short for Electronic Numerical Integrator and Computer), the entire system occupied a large room and needed several people to operate it properly. Vacuum tubes were used to ensure ENIAC functioned properly and that would allow the computer to solve 5,000 problems in one second. It's total weight was about 28 tons (around 56,000 pounds) and it would consume 170,000 watts of power to perform its calculations. Each computer costs around $487,000. By today's price estimates, that would come up to $10 million! It gets worse. The computer featured more than 17,000 tubes to handle, and there was always a situation where a tube would malfunction or would be completely destroyed. Replacing the tubes was no easy matter and was also expensive. In short, it was an expensive, faulty, heavy, and cumbersome machine. Not to mention slow because the computer that you have with you today has about tens of thousands of times the speed of the ENIAC. No one would ever buy a gargantuan machine such as that, and for that reason, it had to be scaled down. A lot.

Eventually, the '70s heralded the birth of the first microcomputer. H. Edward Roberts, who was an ex-Air Force officer, headed a small firm called Micro Instrumentation and Telemetry Systems, or MITS for short. He announced to the world that he was about to launch a microcomputer based around the Intel 8080 micro-processing chip. The microcomputer would meet the demands of the time, and it would be small enough to fit on a table. Named Altair, a photograph of the microcomputer appeared in *Popular Electronics*, a magazine that was read widely by many technology and electronics enthusiasts. The entire computer kit would be sold for $395. Roberts was hoping to simply break even with his computer, aiming to sell around 200 units.

Within just three months of its announcement, Roberts received a total of 4,000 orders.

One of the buyers of the computer was, of course, Bridgewater. As the years progressed, the company would try to get its hands on any of the newer models of microcomputers in the market. It needed them as much as it needed more clients and revenue. After all, it was those computers that set it apart from other companies.

Having learned the hard lesson from his loss, Ray took on a new approach to his work. Every time he started taking a particular position in the market, he would note down the reasons and criteria that led him to take that position. Once the trade was closed, he would go back to his criteria and examine them to see how well they had worked. He also realized that he would need to understand the criteria using actual data. And so, he would convert those criteria into a set of formulas. He would then take historical data and use the formulas on them to check whether his actions in the past were much better than his decisions in the present.

Here is how the entire process worked. He would use his intuition and information to come across an idea or thought. He would then use logical reasons to guide that idea toward a particular decision and note down all the criteria that was used to come to that particular decision. Once the decision had taken place, he would then use formulas that were already entered into the computer to find out how it performed in the present and then compare it a similar decision in the past using the same set of formulas. Based on the results, he would decide if he needed to modify anything or if he was performing well.

He would not only use this to test his own decisions, but economic data from various countries. It allowed Ray to truly understand how to refine his market positions, how to make effective decisions, and, more importantly, find out if he is heading into a pitfall.

The more data he fed into the system, the more information he received in return. Eventually, Ray was able to create an original system of currencies, stock, precious metals, and interest rates based on nearly a century's worth of historical data from various countries and from Ray's past decisions. The system was a Bridgewater original, and it allowed them to make more accurate decisions in the market. However, Ray would not be brash and arrogant this time. He would let the computer run its own calculations while he made his own. In the end, he would check his conclusions with the computer. If he was wrong, then he would examine where he made a mistake, which would eventually turn out to be a factor that he had originally overlooked. The lessons he learned through this new method of measuring things was invaluable. Ray did not stop learning, which was his biggest strength growing up. The only difference here was that he was making sure that none of his emotions would enter the picture.

Ray knew that the computer was capable of compiling multiple criteria and could come to a conclusion faster than anyone could at Bridgewater. Rather than try to beat the computer's speed, which would be a pointless endeavor, Ray and his team would instead discuss their reasons for coming to the conclusions that each of them did. Even if their decisions aligned with the computer's, they would debate at large the thought process that guided those decisions. The main purpose of this was to bring as many logical factors into the thought process as possible.

However, a few things that the computer lacked were the understanding, imagination, and logic that the team could bring to the table, which is why they learned another method that would help them greatly: a combination of their knowledge and tactics with the computer's speedy and accurate processing.

Over the coming decades, this technique would allow them to create a powerful system to understand the market, predict variations and directions of instruments, price patterns, potential investments, and more. Today, Bridgewater not only combines years of incredible data, but also the latest technologies to give their clients an incredible, accurate, and informational service.

But wait. We are fast-forwarding right here. Let's go back to 1983. There is much to be said about that time. More importantly, we have to talk about the resurrection of Bridgewater.

By late 1983, Ray managed to increase the employee strength of Bridgewater to six. For the most part, he had always reached out to potential clients directly. He had never actually thought about marketing the company. But because of the amount of research they had collected and the system they had developed, there was a growing demand for their services. The trick was now to capture that demand and then hopefully convert that into revenue, which made Ray hire the seventh employee of the company: a Bible salesman named Rob Fried.

Fried used a door-to-door approach to sales. It was definitely an odd choice. Nevertheless, Ray's hire would soon turn out to be the golden goose. Over the course of the next year, Bridgewater would add a list of notable clients to their business, including Wellington Management, Provident Capital Management, General Electric, Loomis Sayles, the World Bank, Loews Corporation, and Brandywine.

There were three principle areas of services that Bridgewater was offering back then.

- The first one was providing business and marketing consultancy. They would charge their clients a specific fee structure rather than ask them for a take in their profits.

- Second, they would manage the risk of the companies. Again, they would use a fee structure instead of a profit-sharing criteria.

- Finally, they were selling packages that featured their research.

They would end up working with clients from a plethora of industrial backgrounds. Public utilities, food producers, banks, multinational businesses, and many other forms of governmental, financial, and corporate entities all became part of the Bridgewater portfolio.

Ray had a unique approach to his business. He would become so involved with the company or organization until it reached a point where he was confident that the strategies that the organization was using were something he would personally use if he were heading that particular organization. The approach definitely worked with the clients as they began to develop more trust in Ray's methods. He would also break down the organization into various components and provide sound strategies to manage each component through numerous derivative instruments and financial tools. To Ray, each of his clients was a story about the success of his business. It did not matter who he was working with, he would not accept defeat that easily.

Which is why, when he was working with one of the richest people in Australia, Alan Bond, the result of their business left a mark on Ray. When Bond had approached Ray, he had borrowed large sums of the U.S. dollar to buy numerous assets in Australia. He was betting on the idea that the U.S. dollar would not rise, meaning that he would be able to pay back his loans at a low interest rate. Unfortunately, his predictions were off course, and the U.S. dollar's rates did increase. None of the assets that Bond had were enough to pay off the debts that he found himself in. His team held an emergency meeting and then got in touch with Ray. When Ray arrived, he got down to the laborious task of poring through their company records. He understood that if they placed their bets on other currencies, then they were definitely headed for a loss. He advised them to wait. When the Australian dollar began to show recovery, he advised them to bet against the currency. Unfortunately, the team did not heed Ray's advice. Eventually, the Australian dollar value plunged to such a low that the team called for another emergency meeting. But, by that time, the damage was done and there was nothing that Ray could do. Because he was with the team during their fall, he took the matter personally. It would leave a bitter taste in his mouth and a strong impression in his mind.

Ray realized that the consulting part of the business was taking off faster than the others. It wasn't that the other two products were in less demand or that they were performing poorly. Rather, Ray was able to provide more consultation services to clients, especially after the list of global entities that he was working with kept increasing. His love for travel was still within him, and it was 1984 when he found himself traveling yet again, but this time to Beijing, China. The only reason he was given an invitation to travel was because he had a small office in Hong Kong catering to CITIC, the only business in China that was allowed to interact with the outside world.

Back then, there was no financial market in China. A small group of seven companies, which included CITIC, was formed to solve this problem together. This market, which was then called the Securities Executive Education Council, operated out of a small hotel room with barely any funding. Ray would understand the scope of the business and make a small donation to the firm, even supplying them with the knowledge that he had accumulated over the years.

China would play an important role in Ray's life in the future. He would go on to open Bridgewater China Partners, a profitable but short-lived venture. This was because Ray would find out that running two companies at the same time (Bridgewater and Bridgewater China Partners) would prove to be a challenge. He could either focus on one or end up losing both. He had to make a choice, and that choice involved a sacrifice. He had to let go of Bridgewater China Partners.

By the mid-1980s, there was growth occurring in the company. Bridgewater was now a 10-member strong team. Ray needed more space for the work and ended up renting an old farmhouse. Because of his success with China, he started receiving consultancy work for the governments of Australia, Abu Dhabi, and Singapore. It was also during this time that he started taking his sons on his business trips. A moment that he would remember was when Devon, who was ten years old, brought back silk scarves from China for $1 and sold them in a shopping mall for $20. Ray could already see how business-savvy Devon was. But to Ray, it was not just one son who would be important to him. He considered his family, his extended family, and all the people he worked with important pieces of his life. To him, it was important to strike a balance between work and family.

1986 would be the year that Bob Prince would join Bridgewater when he was still in his twenties. He would go on to become Ray's partner and someone he would call a brother for more than 30 years. Even today, they remain close and Ray considers him to be one of Bridgewater's greatest additions.

Before the end of the 1980s, Bridgewater would grow to a team of 20 people. By then, it was time to face more unpredictable changes in the market.

# Chapter 6: Lessons from Recovery

Believe in the goals and dreams that you have set in life because the alternative would be a life less challenging and less rewarding.

Ray knew that. It was why, when faced with a tough choice to make during the most challenging part of his life, he chose to stick with the company he had built. For him, there was no other alternative. He could not even imagine abandoning the very things that he not only believed in, but had built with all his effort and sacrifice.

No matter who you are, there are going to be moments when things are going to be so overwhelming that it seems easier to take the easy way out. You might have suffered so many repeated setbacks and disappointments that you might start thinking that perhaps it is okay to throw the towel. There is no harm to choosing another path, is there?

Truth be told, there isn't.

But are you making that decision from a calm and logical space, or is your decision going to be largely emotional? When Ray was presented with the fate of his family on the line, his emotions were stretched to their limits. He was going to consider heading back to Wall Street and suiting up for a job that he would not have liked. But he allowed himself to get himself under control. It wasn't that he thought that finding a job was a terrible decision. He just wanted to be absolutely certain that if he took that course in his life, he would be doing so because he had thought things through properly. After carefully putting weight to various reasonings and choices, he realized that he would never let Bridgewater sink. That was what he was good at, and it was something that he could not trade for any other life.

Think about the decisions in your life. When you jump to conclusions, are you are giving each of the decisions the value and consideration that they deserve? There is nothing wrong with taking some time to carefully evaluate what you want out of life. Think of each choice you are about to make and look at where they might take you. Are you happy with the destination? Are you going to be satisfied with what you might have at that point? If you are certain you can live with the results of your decision, then go ahead and make it.

Ray also understood the value of the people in your life. He would never sacrifice the time he got with his family. Relationships mattered to him, and it was for this reason that he focused on building long-lasting relationships with not only the people he worked with, but with the people he encountered in his life.

It is not always about the "what," but also about the "who." Without the people in our lives, everything we have has nothing but a monetary value. It's like all the things that occupy our life have a price tag. There is nothing we can call invaluable or something we can truly say has meaning without having to spend anything on it.

As Ray began to rebuild Bridgewater with the people he valued in his life, he discovered something else. He understood the value of goals. This was a revelation that he had received as he had to let go of Bridgewater China Partners. He realized that while you can have practically anything that you want, it does not mean that you can have everything that you want. There are times when you might have to give up something either to have or to hold on to something else.

Ray understood something about life; it's like giant buffet line with so many options. But you know that you cannot have them all unless you take a small bite out of each one. If you do take a small bite, then you are not fully having something, and nothing happens when you merely decide to take a bite out of something. Sometimes, you need to let go of all the other alternatives and distractions to focus on the one thing that you would like to have the most. The choice is never easy. After all, what if the other items in the buffet line are all inviting and equally wonderful?

You can have more of what you know will make you happy or bits of everything you know will keep you satisfied.

Your choice.

# Chapter 7: Stage of Life: Achieving Liftoff (1988-1995)

1988.

More twists and turns would fill the life of Bridgewater. Each of them would change Ray's views on his life and to the world of investing. He was careful to avoid the pitfalls using the wisdom he gained from all his past experiences. 1988 was a year of little volatility. This cost Bridgewater and the company ended up earning a little more than half of the previous year's earnings. Still, it was nothing they couldn't handle and ended being just one more lesson to learn.

During that time, there were many who worked at Bridgewater who would doubt the systematized manner in which Ray and Bob would approach things. This would become apparent when the system would not work too well. This was an expected setback, and Ray knew that no system, no matter how powerful, could be accurate all the time. There were bound to be errors. He tried to convince his coworkers about the importance and need for the system. Sometimes, he would succeed, but at other times, he would not be able to change their minds. He would understand that such disagreements were all right and were quite frankly, necessary. After all, it was only through such discussions that Ray would find ways to improve. However, what no one could do was change Ray's mind about the system, as no one could provide a viable, logical, and convincing enough reason to make Ray give up on the system he had built.

Despite the decrease in performance in 1988, it was still a great year for Bridgewater. That was because the team was able to discover new lessons from their work and use that in their system, which was only growing more advanced as the years went by.

The '80s were coming to a close. By the end of the decade, Bridgewater was two dozen employees strong. Giselle Wagner, who would go on to manage the investment side of the business for the next twenty years, would join the company in 1988. Two more long-term employees, Dan Bernstein and Ross Waller, would also become part of the Bridgewater team in 1988 and 1989, respectively.

Quite a few of the employees in Bridgewater were fresh out of college with little or no experience. However, what Ray saw in them was the drive to succeed and the hunger to accomplish so much more in their lives. As Ray had himself seen the value of real-world experience and the will to keep on going, he looked for similar traits in the people he hired rather than some knowledge that they were forced to memorize from a textbook.

When they had started handling the accounts of the World Bank, the investment portfolio that they were managing was around $5 million. By the time the new members had joined Bridgewater, the company was officially handling $180 million worth of investments. Their reputation had grown, and companies were willing to trust them more.

That was when Kodak approached Ray.

Before the camera manufacturer would suffer a fall that would go down in the history books, it was a well-reputed global company. In fact, the 1980s started with huge growth for Kodak, with sales reaching a little over $10 billion. This was all before the rise of digital photography and the challenges that new technologies would pose to a company like Kodak that was hell bent on preserving its analog camera technology. Eventually, they would start releasing their version of digital cameras in 1991, but by then, it would be too late, as their customers would have drifted off to other camera manufacturing companies. It was only in the late 1980s that Kodak would realize its mistake and its sales were heading in the wrong direction. One of the things that Kodak did have going for them was their reputation, which they would use to their fullest capability.

Rusty Olson, who was the Chief Investment Officer of Kodak, wanted Bridgewater to take care of a problem that they had with their investments. Ray knew that despite the clients that they had, having Kodak as part of their client list would make a big difference. Such was the fame of the camera manufacturer back then.

Ray would handle Kodak just as he did all of his accounts. He would break the company up in various components and then would apply various financial instruments to figure out a solution. He was so successful at it that he not only impressed Olson, but he returned with a $100 million account.

But despite the success, Ray always remembered his failures. Her recollected how his arrogance and brash nature had nearly sunk his company and sent his family into a terrible financial situation. He would never let that happen again. Despite the many successes, Ray knew that failure was just one mistake away. The answer was that he would not stop taking risks, but he would try and understand those risks to create a careful path ahead of him. He knew that he had to diversify his accounts that featured high-quality returns. This would allow him to reach out to other clients and offer them a unique set of services.

At that time, Ray also knew that he had to innovate the system he had created. He wanted it to become something that Bridgewater could use to lure in more clients. To do so, he went to work with Brian Gold, who had joined Bridgewater in 1990. He wanted to know what would happen to a portfolio if they added more unique investments that had different correlations. How volatile would the portfolio become and how much would its quality improve?

To understand the above concept, let us think about a bowl of fruit salad. The bowl represents a client's portfolio, and all the fruit inside represents their investments. Typically, clients do not like to keep their investments too broad. There is a lot of risk involved and no one knows which way the tides might turn. Even if the investments were diverse, they would focus on one sector, which would make it easier for the investor to focus their attention, which means the investor's bowl would feature only oranges, but they would be various kinds of oranges from around the world. For example, it would feature Jaffa, Valencia, Cara Cara, and Navel oranges. What Ray was proposing was making it even more diverse but still keeping certain correlations between them. For example, his fruit salad would focus on fruits with different correlations, perhaps a mix of sour and mildly sweet fruits. Therefore, his bowl would have strawberries, kiwis, oranges, certain types of apples, watermelon, and maybe even a pineapple thrown in there for good measure. There were definitely a few common themes with the fruit, but they were still diverse to allow for a whole lot of options. However, Ray still wanted to know what would happen if there were such unique investments.

To many of us, this might not have been a very innovative thought. But back then, this was something people were skeptical of trying. Thankfully, Ray had with him a computer inputted with decades of research materials. His calculations would be more accurate and would not be based on mere speculation.

When the results came out, it was a euphoric feeling. Ray thought he knew what Albert Einstein felt when he discovered $E=MC^2$.

Ray would go on to call his discovery the "Holy Grail of Investing" and believed that it would bring him a fortune.

The best part was that Ray knew that this investment method could work on any business, whether it was from the hospitality sector or technology; having a diverse set of income streams would definitely be possible using the method Ray had envisioned. Because he had been documenting and systemizing all of his investments, decisions and results, he could look through so much data spanning decades. This data allowed him to choose different asset classes, test out the product, and make sure they could pick out any problems in the initial stages of its trial period.

Once Ray, Bob, and Dan completed their testing, they would test it again.

And again.

And again for good measure.

Because what they discovered was staggering, and they did not want to be proven wrong. Especially Ray. It was as though he had discovered a treasure chest, and this time he was going to make sure all the gold piled inside the chest was really there and that it was not a trap that would lead them to another pitfall. He was being cautious, his experience kicking in, and his emotions taking a backseat. In fact, his emotions might just be thrown into the trunk and locked away for good measure.

You see, what had surprised the trio was that their method could easily improve their results by three–sometimes as much as five–times for every unit of risk they took. At the same time, they could adjust the return based on the risk that they were going to take. What that meant was that they could make a ton of money without the risks throwing them completely off their game. Ray nicknamed it the "killer system," but he was cautious at the same time. He had been there and seen good things happen only to see it crumble away.

The team was excited, but caution was the name of the game. Initially, they risked only 10% of the investment they were originally planning to make. That way, if things went south, there would not be a huge loss to suffer. They received impressive results and made money based on their investment. Next, they increased their risks a little more, trying to test the waters and thinking that they might eventually reach a limit that they wouldn't be able to cross. The more they tried, the more confident the team became in the product itself. It was time to reach out to potential clients with their new system.

But once again, they wouldn't just blindly request their clients to invest a lot of money into a system no one knew about. So they would only seek out a modest $1 million trial amount from their clients, which was barely a large sum for many of the clients they were dealing with. Ray named the system "Top 5 %" initially because it consisted of results and calculations from the top 5 % of the decisions that they had taken in the past decades. But the name sounded like mouthful and so, Ray would rename the system to Pure Alpha, as all the decisions that comprised the system were like the alphas of the group.

Pure Alpha became the very best way that Bridgewater knew to manage money efficiently. At the same time, the team knew that if they were going to make money out of the product, then they wouldn't be able to approach a lot of clients. They could only pitch the product to those who were willing to risk trying it. This meant approaching clients who wouldn't mind spending a few million dollars on innovation. This would prove to be a challenge because despite their best efforts, Pure Alpha would only constitute about 10% of Bridgewater's total assets.

But Pure Alpha would only be one of the innovations made by the company. In 1991, Bridgewater would not only use their system, but their years of expertise, to become the largest active currency managers in the world—a title that would put their company on the map.

That did not mean that the team was immune to mistakes. They continued to make them, but all the mistakes they committed were within a certain expected range. The days of allowing their mistakes go spiraling out control were long gone.

Ray would also develop a unique approach to dealing with the mistakes of the people who worked with him. In one such incident, the person in charge of trading, Ross, was given the task of putting in a trade for a client. For various reasons, he forgot to do so and the cash was just lying there. Eventually, the oversight was discovered, but not before damage of several hundreds of thousands of dollars occurred.

If Ray was like other managers, he would have fired Ross. But when he thought about it–keeping his emotions aside–he realized that it would set a bad example for the others. In fact, it would encourage others to hide their mistakes. He didn't want people to avoid errors and mistakes. Rather, he wanted to bring problems to the table so that the team could discuss what could be done about them. He set up an "error log" so that anytime someone made a mistake, they would record it in the error log. They would then find solutions to improve the situation. This allowed the team to constantly improve themselves and the efficiency in the company doubled.

Unbeknownst to Ray, he would eventually receive an email that would prove to be a wakeup call. It would change the way he managed things.

In 1993, Dan, Bob, and Giselle would take Ray out to dinner to communicate to him the way he affects the people in the company and their morale. Rather than spontaneously drop him with feedback, they decided to send across an email to him to explain what they were going to focus on. The email started with the positive side of Ray, talking about his energy and intensity. It mentioned how he would always keep high standards and that would not only be reflected in his work but in the people around him. He was a man who allowed flexible working conditions for his staff and team and made sure he compensated them well.

So far, so good.

Then came the part about his negative traits. The team pointed out that sometimes Ray would say or do things that would make the people under him feel belittled, humiliated, incompetent, overwhelmed, and oppressed.

The email was like a sucker punch to Ray. In all the years he had been working with his team, he had never realized that his words and actions had created such consequences. To him, all his employees were like his extended family.

This meant that Ray was presented with another tough choice to make. He could do any of the below:

1) He could become exceptionally honest and encourage everyone else to do the same. This meant that some truths were going to be very difficult to deal with, but it would help address various problems that the company was facing.

2) Focus on making his employees satisfied and happy.

Unlike the previous choices that he had made, Ray knew that this time he had to do something different; he had to take the best of both worlds.

Over dinner, Ray asked Dan, Bob, Giselle to hit him with the whole truth. They responded by saying that they, and those who knew him very well, were never demoralized by his reactions, words, and responses. That was because they knew that he came from a good place and that he meant well. However, those who did not know him would not be able to figure out his intentions. To them, he might just seem dominating, relentless, and sometimes even rude.

When Ray heard this, he decided that it was time to bring about some changes in the way Bridgewater worked. Over the course of the next decade, several principles were laid down, but the three that were considered the most important were the below:

1) No one would hide what they really felt or thought about a situation. People should bring their honest opinions to the table.

2) People should be willing to have discussions and at the same time, understand that sometimes, they might have to change along with the course of the company.

3) If disagreements persisted, use a generally accepted method of reaching a conclusion. For example, by using votes to understand which direction or choice was preferred by most people in the team.

With that, Ray was ready to steer Bridgewater along a new course.

# Chapter 8: Lessons from Liftoff

One of the important lessons that Ray learned during this period was that people are wired differently. But that difference should not frighten anyone. Rather, it is an asset to the organization.

With different insights and opinions, there was scope for more growth and innovation in an organization. What Ray discovered was that people are born with attributes that can benefit and hurt them. There is not a person on the planet who has only one of the two. The trick was to recognize the strengths and work with them. It was the way to bring out the potential in people. It was for this reason that he never relied on someone's grades to tell him about their potential. He wanted to see how they implemented their strengths in practice.

It was like creating baseball cards. You pick a player and then give them certain attributes. Eventually, a picture of the person's capabilities are formed. Using those capabilities, you can create a team with skills that complement each other. It was the same with Ray. He understood his team's capabilities and arranged them in various departments.

When he was given the choice between either creating a framework that worked on brutal honesty or establish an environment that would take into consideration employee satisfaction and happiness, Ray realized something else. He understood that you don't have to sacrifice principles for team synergy. Both can be achieved together. It all depends on how you were planning on going about it. Ray had found the right balance between the two, but he couldn't have done it on his own.

It took the people close to him to make him realize that.

And that brings us to another important lesson. Listen to the people who know you and think about their feedback in a logical manner. Analyze them to see how much weight they hold. If there is a semblance of truth to their words, then think about how you can use that to improve yourself.

Some truths are difficult to face. But by facing them, you only give yourself more opportunities to grow.

# Chapter 9: Stage of Life: Coming to the Crossroads (1995- 2003)

1995.

At this point, Bridgewater had grown into a medium-sized company with about forty-two employees working full-time. Their collective asset management amounted to $4.1 billion. This position was beyond Ray's expectations considering the fact that he had to borrow money from his father just to make ends meet just a decade or so ago.

Despite the growth, Ray felt that the team was doing nothing new or was not innovating themselves enough. Sure, they had developed a system that could help them with their clients' accounts, but he felt that Bridgewater was capable of more.

That was why he decided that while he and his team were capable of handling the data that they received, it was slowly becoming more complex. He needed to bring fresh minds to the table. He then hired young programmers who were better than anyone on the Bridgewater team at converting many of the company's instructions into codes. Once again, Ray was not looking at people who had years of experience. He hired fresh graduates; people fresh off the boat but with tons of potential and drive.

One of the young grads who joined his team was Greg Jensen. He started working at Bridgewater as an intern in 1996. He showed so much potential that Ray had no choice but to promote him as a research assistant. Over the years, Greg contributed so much to the company and its growth that he was eventually raised to become the co-Chief Investment Officer along with Bob and Ray. But that did not stop Greg from achieving more. He kept at it, creating even better milestones for the company. This is what led him to eventually become the co-CEO of the company. He would also become a godson to Ray.

Together, the three of them would go on to invest in even more powerful companies. With Greg's help, they were able to bring more data into their systems to eventually analyze things from a higher perspective.

It was also during this time that Ray began to consider establishing a trust for his family. With his extensive knowledge, he began to look at the best possible mix of assets that would allow the wealth to be preserved over generations, without being affected too much by inflation and other market factors.

He would not include cash because he knew how much value it would lose if one accounts for inflation. Then there was the situation of taxes, which would further diminish the value of the cash at a future date. And so, he brought in Dan and Bob to bring together a portfolio mix that would not just survive the next decade, but the next hundred years or so. He would call it the "All Weather Portfolio" because he was certain that it could perform well in any economic environment.

Initially, it was an instrument that only Bridgewater was managing. After all, it was for Ray's family and it wasn't exactly something he wanted to sell as a product. But then he arrived at another crossroads. It was in 2003, and the head of Verizon's pension fund was looking into creating an investment portfolio that could perform well in any condition. At that time, Ray only knew of one such portfolio.

Would he share it?

# Chapter 10: Lessons from Crossroads

Ray understood something big about hiring people. He knew that the wrong hire could cause any company huge penalties. But how was Ray able to pick out good people so well? Did he have a secret technique that others did not know about?

Hardly.

You see, during the initial period of Bridgewater's hiring process, he would hire people he liked. But many of those hires would eventually turn out to be bad decisions. Since Ray and others liked the people they hired, it would be difficult to let them go. They had to find a solution. Eventually, they started to analyze resumes. They looked for certain skills and evaluated how well someone's experience reflected their work experience. Though even that turned out to be a wrong way to hire people because they would find even more bad apples. This does not mean that they were never able to hire good employees. It just meant that their hiring process needed to be refined even more. It was then that they realized that the problem was not with the resumes, but with the questions that they were asking the interviewees. They resorted to what every other employer decided to ask people who came in for interviews. The questions that were asked were based on biased perspectives of the team at Bridgewater. It was time to broaden their way of thinking.

They soon discovered a more robust hiring process that would incorporate two essential factors:

1) The hiring team would be honest and clear about what exactly they were looking for in the person they would like to add to their team. This would allow them to not only manage expectations but would narrow down the candidates to those who fit the requirements.

2) Their focus would not only be on the number of years someone had on their resume. It would focus on the person's knowledge, drive, goals, and other factors that would allow the hiring team to focus on abilities at a more granular level.

They did not want people who were only good at following orders. They wanted team members who could think independently and were not afraid to add more value to the overall growth of Bridgewater. They wanted people who were not afraid to seek out excellence and were not deterred by competition.

At the same time, Ray was looking for people who were capable of putting aside their egos. He knew personally how much damage emotions and egos could cause, having lived through it himself. He wanted people who would take a pragmatic approach to things.

The process of hiring is never easy. One has to look through countless people before they are able to narrow it down to the right person for the job.

This was something Ray would also find out to be true in real life. When we surround ourselves with friends, we often tend to add as many people as possible into our lives. But if we are aiming to succeed, then we cannot be held back by anyone. When we evaluate our friends, we need to ask ourselves a few important questions. Will the friends we have support us in our journey toward success, or would they rather hold us back because of petty emotions like envy? Can we trust our friends to celebrate our success and be with us during our failures? More importantly, can we expect our friends to be there during all the difficult phases of our lives?

When we want to accomplish goals, it is important that we surround ourselves with like-minded people.

# Chapter 11: Rapid Growth (2003-2006)

2003.

Ray had the answer for Verizon. He would share the details of the portfolio that he had created. Verizon was interested and immediately made their investment. Once the initial investment was made, other big companies and global entities followed suit.

It was a period of rapid growth because Bridgewater found themselves managing an astounding $80 billion.

At the same time, Ray had another thought in his head. The company was growing. There was so much potential that they could take advantage of. What would they do about their identity?

He did not want them to continue being a boutique-sized investment management company. That would mean that those clients who wanted someone to manage incredibly large portfolios would look at their company size and think twice about approaching them for advice. Of course, Bridgewater's reputation superseded them. But with that reputation came the responsibility of creating an image that matched the position that Bridgewater held.

Additionally, Ray knew that if they grew, they could make use of better technology, much more advanced security features, and a deeper pool of talent. All of these resources would allow Bridgewater to become not just an institution with long-term growth capabilities, but with greater stability as well.

Bridgewater began to grow even more.

In 2006, there were even more managers in the organization. At that time, the problem was not finding new talent. It was getting them acclimated to the company culture and values. From the moment Ray had received feedback from Dan, Bob, and Giselle, he was constantly adding more important values to the list of principles that he had set about for the company. This was why, in the same year, Ray had an extensive list of nearly 60 principles that he circulated among the managers of the company. His aim was not to force them into accepting them. In fact, when he sent out the principles, he mentioned the fact that they were just rough drafts. He wanted the managers to look at the principles and debate them. He wanted them to challenge them if they needed to be challenged.

And thus began the process of aligning the leaders and managers on the principles that would help them grow together, meet challenges as a team, and help focus on the growth of the company. Eventually, the number of principles would not lessen, but increase even more. When it was done, Ray had established a list of what he called the "Work Principles" of Bridgewater that encompassed nearly 100 principles. While some may be of the opinion that the list was rather extensive, no one could deny the fact that it brought Bridgewater employees together and allowed them to work in as much synergy as possible.

However, while the process of establishing principles allowed Bridgewater to communicate the core message of their approach to work, progress, and teamwork, it could not explain the Bridgewater philosophy. That would require a different kind of approach.

Ray discovered one such approach. He decided that he would make practically all meetings available to the Bridgewater team. While some meetings were highly confidential and could not be revealed to everyone, Ray made sure that as many meetings involving the leadership team were available for the rest of the organization's members to view and understand. In the beginning, Ray would practically send all the meetings in an unedited format to everyone. He later realized that such a format would be a drain on people's time. And so, he created a small team to edit the recordings and then send them in an easily accessible and easily digestible format to everyone.

The approach produced some interesting results. Team members began to develop more frank discussions about their work and each other. Hidden agendas and petty disagreements began to be resolved faster. Seeing the leader of the organization live the very principles that he talked about encouraged others to do the same.

At the same time, Ray turned his attention to psychology.

# Chapter 12: Lessons from Rapid Growth

When Ray had initially suggested the idea of expansion, Giselle was against it. She felt that it would stretch the office culture too thin. In other words, they would start adding people who might not easily adjust to the office culture.

Ray understood that risk. But what he knew even more is that change is inevitable.

What he wanted to do was make Bridgewater bigger, and the only way to do that was to understand that they could not be a boutique firm anymore. They had to become a proper organization. This presented Ray with many challenges. They had to hire even more talent and get them used to the company culture and philosophy.

But challenges are not roadblocks.

Just because something takes a little more effort to establish does not mean that one should skip it entirely. No effort to expand and grow is going to go without putting in the right degree of effort. Ray had a few rules he lived by when he had to make some important decisions.

- Make sure that you know who you ask questions to. There are people who are capable of giving you sound advice, and there are those who just throw random pieces of information at you. Even when you ask questions, make sure that in the end, you are the one making the final decision. Just because someone says something does not mean it has to be true. Take the time to evaluate the options based on logic and reason.

- Not everything you hear is worth believing. Make sure that you fact-check and come to your own conclusions. For example, if someone tells you that you need to invest $10,000 in gold today because you stand a chance to earn nearly $100,000 in profits, then make sure that you verify the information. When it comes to advice, remember to first examine if the advice is related to the issue you are facing.

- Things always look bigger up close. This means that many things that are happening to you right now might look bigger than they would in retrospect. For example, you might start panicking about something that you might consider to be a truly nerve-wracking situation. But upon reflection in the future, you might realize that you had no reason to panic after all.

Take a step back. Breathe. Take a moment to collect yourself and have a broader perspective on the situation. You might find something you might have missed earlier.

- Don't try to refine the dots. In life, you might often find yourself breaking a big situation or problem down into smaller components. But don't try too hard to simplify things. You might eventually complicate matters so much that you are focused on numerous things and adding more stress than you realized. When you find out that you are capable of tackling the problem, go ahead. You might face challenges while facing the problem, but that does not mean you should stop and try to make things even simpler. In fact, you might just find out that the process of simplifying things is even more stressful than just trying to solve them.

Don't be afraid of growing. But make sure that you maintain some important principles as you do so.

# Chapter 13: Stage of Life: Psychological Revelations (2006-2008)

2006.

When his children were still young, Ray had them go through psychological evaluations.

To make sure that he wasn't using the services of just any psychologist, he consulted with Sue Quinlan, who came with a lot of recommendations. What he discovered was that her assessments were extremely accurate, and it would help the children have a guide on how they can develop themselves in the years to come.

After seeing the success it had on his children, Ray decided to go through the process himself. He wanted to use her expertise to not only focus on himself, but on the people who worked with him. He took the Myers-Briggs Type Indicator (MBTI) assessment test and discovered that the results it produced were accurate.

The MBTI is one of the most popular tools for self-assessment and personality evaluation. Initially discovered by a mother-daughter team consisting of Katharine Cook Briggs and Isabel Briggs Myers, the

MBTI took heavy inspiration from the works of Carl Jung. Katherine Briggs believed that the various aspects of Jung's studies and discoveries could be translated into a practical approach. The duo then translated Jung's research material into 16 personality types, where each personality was further divided into four personality tendencies or preferences. This allowed people to look at their personalities from a detailed perspective.

The MBTI also included four broad dichotomies that would play a central role in the personality assessment of people. There four dichotomies are:

- Extraversion-Introversion
- Intuition-Sensing
- Thinking-Feeling
- Judging-Perceiving

Both mother and daughter were of the belief that each person behaved in a specific manner as highlighted by one of the 16 classifications of the MBTI. As the popularity of the personality assessment test grew, it would come to be used in many Fortune 500 companies for the purposes of teamwork, motivation, general assessment, conflict resolution, and even personality development.

This was eventually the aim that Ray wanted to achieve. Apart from sending out meeting materials, he wanted to know if there were ways he could effectively resolve disagreements and conflicts within the organization. He wanted to understand his team even more, enabling him to recognize their personalities on a deeper level. When he originally proposed the idea to the team, there wasn't the wholehearted acceptance that he had hoped to receive. Regardless, he was not deterred. At the same time, Ray also wanted to look at other tests that he could use in the organization. This would be a challenge because when psychologists stuck with a particular method, they were reluctant to endorse any other test or technique.

By using his connections, Ray was eventually able to get a hold of Bob Eichinger, a brilliant psychologist who would point Ray to a number of different tests that he could make use of.

It was in early 2008 that he asked all the managers of Bridgewater to take the test. What he discovered was rather astounding. He realized that most of the managers thought exactly as was prescribed by the MBTI test. He would eventually ask the other people in the organization to take the test as well, allowing for him to better understand them.

Ray wanted to eventually connect the dots between the results that he was seeing and the people who were achieving them. This was because he noticed that people would schedule meetings in the same manner, using the same focus and mentality, only to eventually produce the same results. When digging deeper, he discovered that people were made to focus on areas that weren't their strengths. For example, people who did not have a lot of creativity were given tasks that required them to be creative, and those who were not good with details were given detailed-oriented tasks. He needed to devise a way to make sure that each person was allowed to focus on his or her strengths.

This would lead him to develop baseball cards for the people who worked with him. Each of the baseball cards would provide a list of stats. The main theory behind the development of the baseball cards was to pass them around to the management team so that they could pick the right person for the job. Tasks could be distributed to those people who were capable of matching their requirements.

As with all ideas, his proposal to develop the baseball cards was met with resistance. Nobody wanted to be represented in the form of stats. Additionally, one of the biggest concerns was that the cards would not be able to identify the people accurately or measure their capabilities to their full potential. Furthermore, it there were concerns about the fact that developing them would be too time consuming and might serve to segregate people into small groups. It could potentially create divisions in the team or department.

However, Ray was adamant about its success and, eventually, people began to see the benefit of the cards. In fact, most realized that it was better to have their stats displayed out in the open. That way, they wouldn't have to hide their strengths and would not be given tasks or assignments that they were either not capable of doing or were not responsible for. Eventually, people became comfortable just being themselves rather than pretending to have certain skills that others might have assumed that they had.

And then the financial crisis struck the world.

# Chapter 14: Lessons from Psychology

Ray discovered useful insights about himself through self-evaluation. Sure, he did approach a psychologist to help him figure out certain aspects about himself, but through those evaluations, he discovered a few insights about himself that he still uses today. He understands the value of self-evaluation and believes that people should be honest about themselves and their capabilities.

It was the reason why he had developed baseball cards to evaluate people and their stats. He wanted to have a clear picture of his employees and managers.

Many people do not like to know more about themselves. Just like Ray's employees, people are worried that they might not like the results. But that is merely a situation of short-sightedness because it would only serve to encourage the people to ignore all the important characteristics that comprise their personas.

Self-awareness has many components to it. It is partly attributed to emotional intelligence. In fact, people with high emotional intelligence are more aware of themselves. At the same time, it also involves critical thinking. You evaluate yourself from a logical perspective.

This allows you to be openly critical about certain aspects of your personality. This does not mean that you are devaluing yourself. Rather, you are providing constructive criticism about certain aspects of your nature so that you find ways to improve yourself. Self-awareness allows you to account for your strengths and your weaknesses. It also takes into consideration your motivations and feelings.

But why is that important? For one, you know your capabilities.

When Ray discovered the stats of his employees and managers, he was able to distribute tasks more effectively. That way, those who were capable of tackling a project in a particular manner were allowed to do so. In the same way, when you are aware of your strengths and weaknesses, you won't try too hard to do anything that you are not good at. For example, let us assume that you are a creative person. However, while looking for jobs online, you came across a position in the sales department that provided a higher salary than the job role you were earlier looking for. You think that all you might need is some training and you will be ready to tackle the sales job. You head over to the interview and pass it with flying colors. A week later, you have started your new job. A month later, you have performed so poorly and you feel as though you cannot take another moment of the job that you are almost certain that the next time you are invited to the manager's office, it is so you can receive the proverbial boot out of the premises. But if you had chosen the profession that you were good at, then perhaps you would have slowly improved your way to a promotion.

By understanding your capabilities, you are not looking to demotivate yourself. Rather, you are aiming to find out how you can use them to your advantage.

A little self-assessment is always important when you are on the path to achieving your goals.

# Chapter 15: Stage of Life: Financial Crisis (2008-2010)

2008.

The financial crash would change a lot of things. Even at Bridgewater, there would be a transformative period.

Back in the 2000s, Bridgewater had included a depression gauge in their systems. The purpose of this gauge was to evaluate specific actions and combinations of events to predict whether they would indicate a state of heightened debt or depression. In other words, the system was programmed to predict a financial crisis.

In 2007, the system showed some interesting readings. According to the data compiled, there would be a bubble of debt that was really close to bursting wide open and sending the country—and the world—into a financial crisis.

As soon as Ray became aware of the results, he remembered the events of the '80s, when he was so certain that the economy would enter a debt period, but he was eventually proven wrong. Despite the fact that had thirty more years of experience, he was still not confident enough to make the same call again. He was worried that the events of the time would repeat themselves. After the failure to accurately predict the debt situation in the '80s, Ray began to learn more about debt in general.

The experience of the debt situation in the '80s compelled Ray to look more into debt situations in general. He began to uncover details about the Latin-American debt situation in the 1980s. He then turned his attention to Japanese debt situation that occurred in the 1990s. He also read as much as he could about the dot-com bubble that happened in 2000. In fact, he managed to gather information from old journals, newspapers, and other databases about the Great Depression as well. The more he learned, the more he understood.

Back in those days, the financial industry was deregulated. This meant that they were relatively free to create various kinds of financial instruments and products that did not have a lot of oversight. This did not mean that the banks could do anything they wanted, but they had so many different types of loans and credit options that were not examined closely by any authorized institution. This allowed the banks to trade in hedge funds with derivatives. What does that mean? To understand that, we need to gain an understanding of the term "hedge fund."

A hedge fund is a special institution that comprises privately owned companies. Their main goal is to pool together the money of their investors and put them into complicated financial instruments. The main aim of the hedge fund is to outperform the market. Because if they do that, they would not only be able to provide their clients with a good return on their investment, but also be able to increase their own profit margins. It's a win-win situation.

But what about "derivatives"? What does that mean? In short, a derivative is a financial contract where a buyer decides to buy a particular asset on a particular date at a particular price. A simple example would be when someone comes to you with a contract that says that you can buy a house on December 18, 2020 for $18 million. You sign the contract and with that, the deal has been settled. That way, no matter what happens in the economy, you are not going to be paying for any risk. The price of that asset will still remain $18 million at the time of the purchase.

At that time, banks themselves started working like hedge funds. They would pool together the money of various investors into derivatives. Banks started offering mortgages to people at an alarming rate. In fact, they also began to lower the rates on these mortgages. Eventually, there were too many people in the economy with mortgages, and the housing prices began to rise. People had bought the assets, but they were unable to make the payments on the rising rates. Homeowners were suddenly struck with payments that they couldn't make. Eventually, people started defaulting on those mortgages. They began to sell their homes at considerably lower prices than when they had bought them. The housing market bubble finally burst.

In 2008, after studying various debt situations, Ray was certain that the economy was going toward a collapse. He even asked many people to poke holes in his theory and come up with proof to contradict his findings. At the same time, he began to have various conversations with policy makers. His goal was to run his findings through as many filters as possible. He wanted to be absolutely certain that what he had discovered was eventually going to happen and would not lead him to appear on television again and make another false claim. If he did, he wasn't sure that his reputation would ever recover. People can chalk up one mistake to a gross misunderstanding of the market. But two mistakes might convince everyone that there is a pattern of behavior. One that seems to lead to a case of wrongful predictions.

Once Ray realized that his predictions were not in error, he began to get in touch with his clients and prepare their portfolios. The way he did this was by balancing their positions in such a manner that there would be a limited downside and a considerable upside. At the same time, he began to create backup plans for many of the clients in case his predictions were not going to come true again. The idea that the world's economy would fall was scary to everyone at Bridgewater. It would create a long-term effect, and the repercussions would cascade to other economies in such a way that it would cripple them.

In 1982, policymakers had turned their attention to Bridgewater because of the analysis that Ray had provided back during the day (which he had also published). The same situation would occur again. Tim Geihner, who was the president of the New York Fed, invited Ray to meet with him. Along with Greg, Bob, and a young analyst by the name of Bob Elliot, Ray met with Geihner over lunch. As Ray began to walk Geihner through the numbers, he began to look more and more astonished. By the time the team had concluded their reports, the president of the New York Fed had literally turned pale. Something of this magnitude was unheard of.

Two days later, the global investment bank Bear Stearns, collapsed. At that time, not a lot of people paid attention to the situation. Just another business running out of business. However, Ray and his team knew better. They had already predicted that it was about to get much worse for everyone.

Six months later, Lehman Brothers, a global financial services firm also collapsed. Once that happened, it was like tipping over one domino and watching the rest of them fall. One by one, financial institutions and global firms began to crumble under the weight of global financial meltdown.

But for Bridgewater, things were secure. They had predicted the fall and had anticipated the move made by the market. They were able to navigate the economic collapse without incurring much damage, both for them and their clients.

The key takeaway for Ray from the experience was that he had not allowed fear to stop him from doing what he knew best. But at the same time, he approached the entire situation with a sense of wisdom and keenness that he had not previously possessed.

The success of Bridgewater's campaigns put them in the sights of major U.S. policymakers. They were finally ready to receive the Bridgewater treatment for managing funds and measuring economic situations. Though whenever they got in touch with Ray, it was not so much a meeting as it was the policymakers asking him questions and him answering them. What these policymakers wanted was a different perspective on the economy. Investors and investment management firms think in terms of risks. They are usually anticipating things that haven't occurred yet and are willing to place risks to get rewards. On the other hand, policymakers play the safe game. They are not allowed to take too many risks. Every action they performed was controlled and restricted. However, if they had the viewpoints of investors, then they would be able to approach their decisions with better insights and predictions. Additionally, policymakers were often battling their opponents. Even if they were extremely openminded and clear-sighted, they are usually lost in dealing with the opposition and other policies that come their way on a daily basis. Hiring an investment management firm like Bridgewater is like having an extra pair of eyes to monitor the economic situations of the world and, more importantly, the country itself.

But despite the bad market, nothing could beat the returns that Bridgewater gained.

In 2010, they had experienced their best returns ever. They had accumulated a return of over 45% on Pure Alpha and over 18% on All Weather (which was the portfolio that Ray had originally meant to design only for his children). The systems they had used to collect and process information had been constantly accumulating and understanding data since the '80s. It was now a superb machine capable of high degrees of accuracy. The systems were indeed Bridgewater's greatest assets. Without them, the team would have to do things the old fashioned way: by manually looking at all the markets, their influences, and the entire portfolio of investments. That would not only be time-consuming, but it would never have predicted the economic situation of 2008 fast enough. To Ray, the old ways of reading investments were like going through a map, while the use of systems meant that one was equipped with a state-of-the-art GPS.

When Bridgewater's success grew, their clients refused to take their money back because they wanted their money to grow.

# Chapter 16: Lessons from Crisis

Ray understood that once he had built his system, his next step was to improve it. Over the years, he used a 5-step process to bring about improvement in the system.

1) Identify company goals

2) List the problems

3) Diagnose the problems until the root cause was found

4) Design valuable changes or discover solutions

5) Perform the required action

As Bridgewater grew, Ray would ask himself what his next set of goals were. He would understand them and list all of the problems that could result. He would diagnose the problems until he found the root cause, which would eventually point him in the direction of the information that he needed. This information would be fed into the system. He would go about creating possible changes, if they were required, or make decisions. The system would also come to a certain conclusion. He would compare his ideas with the system and then see where he needed to improve. Finally, he would make the decision. That is what allowed him to predict the economy in 2008.

Of course, in life we wish we had a machine that could take in the data, take some measurements, and let us know what the right decision is.

Sadly, such technology has not been invented yet. But until then, there is something else that we can do ourselves. We can use the 5-step method in our lives and keep on improving ourselves.

The steps are simple:

1) We understand what goals we are trying to achieve. For example, let us say that we are looking to improve our financial position.

2) We list all the problems that prevent us from achieving that position. It could be the debts we have to settle, our current job position, or even the lack of financial support.

3) We try and think about the root cause of all our problems. In this case, most of the other problems can be solved if we aimed to find a better job position.

4) Find out the solutions. We go ahead and apply to various organizations. We update our resume and seek out better job opportunities.

5) Finally, we take the action required.

When you approach your life through a step-by-step logical process, you realize that it becomes much easier for you to evaluate problems and discover the right solutions.

# Chapter 17: Going Public/Publishing Principles (2010-2011)

2010.

Ray believes that there are three phases of life.

In the first, we are dependent on others. But that is okay because it is a learning phase and the more we learn, the more understanding we have about the world around us. Besides, we do need a foundation in our lives.

The second phase is where others depend on us because of our work. We are usually in an employee, or perhaps managerial, position. But at that time, someone is looking at us to deliver results. But even if you were, say, the CEO of a vast global firm, many still depend on you. In fact, the organization or business entity depends on you to bring it to a level where it can run on its own with minimal interference from you.

The final phase is where there is nothing or no one dependent on you. You are free to savor the finer things in life.

At the time, Ray was holding two positions at Bridgewater and he wanted to get out of both of them. He was managing the company as a whole in the role of Chief Executive Officer, and he was managing the various investments of the company as Chief Investment Officer. He didn't want to be needed for both positions.

One of the biggest concerns that Ray faced was whether he should leave the company entirely or if he should stay behind in the capacity of a mentor. He liked the idea of stepping away from the leadership role because that would mean that whoever would enter his position would have the freedom to continue moving the company forward under a new vision. Also, no one likes having someone looking over their shoulder, which would happen if Ray was still around. However, it was not like Ray had many transitions before. He was unsure of how to proceed. In fact, he was skeptical about it all. Eventually, Ray decided that he would stay on in a mentorship capacity, where he would not interrupt the decisions. Rather, he would be there if someone needed his advice.

Ray and his team agreed that if there was going to be a transition, it should happen quickly so that anyone who would be taking over would have enough time to gain experience and make any small adjustments if it was necessary. The team knew that the transitioning process wouldn't take just a few months or a year. It could go on for two, five, or maybe even ten years.

On January 1, 2011, Ray stepped down as the CEO and handed over the responsibilities to David McCormick and Greg Jensen.

Of course, over the period of the next eighteen months, the new management struggled to find sure footing with their work. But the team looked at all the problems that they faced in the way that they approached all their clients. They would break down the problem into smaller components and try to find a solution for them. One of the factors that would always become part of a company or organization when a new management team takes over is the introduction of new ideas, techniques, and processes. When Greg and David took control, they needed a set of foundational guidelines that would help them navigate. They turned to Ray, who eventually put down all his attributes of how he ran the company, the thought processes he had, and the way he would analyze things. This collection of attributes was nicknamed the "Ray gap." It is important to know that the name wasn't chosen out of vanity. In fact, if any of the others—Bob, Greg, or David—were leaving, then a gap with their name would be created to collect all their attributes. Since it was Ray who was departing the company, he would leave his wisdom for others to follow.

The "Ray gap" would also be known as a "shaper." According to Ray, a shaper is someone who has a bold vision and shapes something iconic, ignoring all the opposition and doubts that others put in their way. His favorite shaper was Steve Jobs, but he recognized the others who were about to make their mark in the current generation. Jeff Bezos, Elon Musk, Geoffrey Canada, and Reed Hastings were some he named in the world of business and organization. When it came to governments and leaders of countries, he would name Lee Kuan Yew and Winston Churchill as his inspirations.

Having understood the work of shapers and the mark they make in history, Ray wanted to identify those who would become the shapers of Bridgewater.

With that goal in mind, Ray would hand over his responsibilities over to a new generation of leaders.

# Chapter 18: Lessons from Going Public

Ray began to have more conversations with other shapers.

What he noticed was that shapers do not let anything come between them and their goals. Their mental fortitude is strong, and they are entirely focused on the goals they would like to achieve. They have strong emotional intelligence, and they are ready to take on any challenges head on. Shapers are able to assess the bigger picture and also able to understand things on a micro scale. When most people can only see one path in front of them, shapers look at multiple paths and are constantly changing directions to pick the best route to get to their destination. Most importantly, they are passionate about what they do.

However, one thing that Ray noticed about shapers is the fact that they would rank really low in one particular category.

Concern for others.

It does not matter who the shaper is or what they have done. Some of the examples that Ray cites are those of Muhammad Yunus, who received the Nobel Peace Prize for his ideas on microfinance and microcredit. Yet he was often tested as low on "concern for others." The same would go to Bill Gates and Geoffrey Canada, who would go on to do more for the disadvantaged children in New York City. It seemed that regardless of what they did, the shapers would test as having a low concern for others. Ray began to wonder. Why was it so? Why did all these people score low on "concern for others" despite their actions showing otherwise?

Ray then came to an important realization. When it came to a choice between creating an impression on others and achieving something, shapers always chose the option to achieve something. This, he realized, should be something people should follow if they would like to achieve their dreams.

When you are faced with chasing your dreams, you need to combine your dreams with your reality. In fact, this was something he points out in his social media posts as well, which he updates regularly with ideas and messages that he had learnt over the course of his career.

# Chapter 19: European Debt Crisis (2010-2016)

2010.

The Bridgewater system was pointing toward another looming debt crisis. And this time, it would strike the continent of Europe. The team was trying to compare the scenario with their calculations during the 2008 crisis.

Once again, Ray was careful. From the lessons learned from the 1980 and 2008 debt crises, he understood that if he needed to be right again, he would have to go through the same careful process he had undertaken during the previous successful prediction. He wanted to be right. It would be a big deal and would drive the company in a new direction. Their previous success had caught the eye of the policymakers in the U.S. One could only imagine the success that a European assignment would bring.

Ray used the same tactics as he had during the 2008 financial crisis. It had helped him, and he could see no reason to abandon the process. He approached policymakers and then asked them to refute his idea. He did encounter resistance, but he was not provided one good reason why he was wrong. The problem was that things were relatively stable in that year. The world had realized that Greece could possibly default on its debt in 2009. To prevent the default and send the economy crashing down, the EU provided addition loans to Greece to continue making its payments. As of 2019, Greece had only managed to pay back a little over 41 billion euros. And that is still not enough. The debt payment scheme has been scheduled to continue beyond 2060. In fact, the situation reached such a low point for Greece that it had to cease the production of its currency, drachma, which was in existence since the mid-6th century and contained one of the oldest coins in the world. Because of the debt settlement scheme provided by the EU, Greece had no option but to adopt the euro as its main currency, ceasing the production of the drachma.

But since the problem was with just one country, the world thought that the worst was over. The alternative was a situation that no one wanted to think about. They had too much to lose and too few solutions to deal with the repercussions of an economic fallout. However, Ray had analyzed the debt situation of Europe and predicted that many other countries would end up not paying their debts, especially since these very debts were accumulated over a period of years.

Greece was just the beginning. Eventually, Portugal, Italy, Spain, and Ireland would follow.

But was debt the only problem? Couldn't Greece pay back the debt easily?

To understand this, we have to turn back the clock slightly. And by slightly, we just have to look back at the financial crisis in the U.S. After the economy bombed and the rest of the world felt the repercussions, there was a slow growth of economy around the world. What the financial crisis also managed to do was reveal some of the fiscal policies of many countries. It revealed the flaws that these policies had in them. That was why the fiscal policies of Greece were rather poorly created. They were focused more on spending and less on paying back their debts. For years, Greece had been putting expenses into various areas without thought or reason. There were no reforms made to their policies. When the big crash had occurred, they were the first to feel the effect of slow economic growth. In 2009, Prime Minister George Papandreou even made a public announcement stating that the previous government had failed to reveal the extent of the nation's deficit. But nothing anyone said could change the course that the country was taking.

In 2010, Greece was forced to request help from the International Monetary Fund (IMF).

The IMF released an astounding $163 billion to help Greece out of the debt situation it had put itself in. As the policymakers of Greece began to discuss strategies, they realized that the money lent to them was not enough. It was time for additional funds.

A second bailout was made in 2011.

The sum? $157 billion.

Ireland and Portugal were two other countries that received bailouts as well to help with their economic situation. Eventually, Italy and Spain could not afford the economic disaster that they were headed into. In December 2011, it was estimated that collectively, all five countries received bailouts equivalent to the sum of $639 billion, with Greece receiving the highest percentage among them.

Many people might recommend that countries simply walk away from their debts. But the reality of the situation is not that easy. Everything is interconnected. If a country tries to simply skip its debts, then the value of its bonds will plunge. Eventually, the banks of the country will then show a sharp reduction in the number of assets in their balance sheet. This means that the liabilities that the banks have will increase tremendously. Eventually, the country might have to call for insolvency. In other words, they have to say that they cannot pay their debts back at all. If a particular company declares insolvency, then its assets will be sold and the company will cease functions.

If Greece had decided to declare insolvency, then the country could have possibly been erased off of the map.

For Ray, there was only one clear conclusion, and this time, he was certain of it. There was just one small problem: convincing people of the facts. You see, what Ray explained painted a grim picture, and nobody liked listening to or knowing about news that was so bad, so it was unheard for a long time. Ray based all his conclusions on the system he had created and his careful analysis of the market. The people who he spoke to thought of the market as a case study, similar to how academics would discuss something in a school setting. One of the examples of this was the fact that they collectively grouped together investors as "the market," rather than thinking of them as different entities, individuals, and organizations that were capable of changing a specific market, such as stocks, currencies, and so on.

But Ray persisted. He knew that he had all the facts. It was only a matter of getting the policymakers and officials to see it. Eventually, he got the governments to change their opinions and see things his way. That was when he hit another roadblock. While the political decision-making systems were swayed by Ray's facts, they would find making a decision a challenging matter. This is because each member country of the European Union had to agree with each other before any action could take place. Sometimes, decisions had to be agreed upon unanimously, especially if it concerned the collective economies of the member countries. Even after that, there are many stages of decision-making.

In a typical decision-making process, the member countries (usually represented by the Heads of State) first debate and then come to a particular agreement. The Commission of the EU begins to create proposals for new laws, which are eventually sent across to The Parliament. At this point, the Council of Ministers and the Parliament both work to pass the decision, and together they approve the laws. Once the laws have been enacted, the Commission then makes sure that they are followed. Any disagreements that may arise are settled in the European Court of Justice.

The long and thorough process is necessary. After all, nations are collectively getting together to make economic and political decisions. However, this would mean that Ray had to wait longer to see the results of his endeavor.

Eventually, word got out about Ray's predictions. Within eighteen months, he began to meet with numerous policymakers from across the European nations. The EU could not ignore the situation unfolding around them anymore. It was a big win for Bridgewater, having finally connected with various important decision-makers around the world.

In 2015, Bridgewater turned forty. It was an incredible milestone, and Ray celebrated it at the office. People who had stayed for a long time in the company came on stage to speak about the journey and what they had learned during the process of building the company. It was also the time that Ray had made the decision to complete his transition of leaving the company.

It was an emotional moment, but Ray knew that it might become a little more difficult over the course of the next year or so.

# Chapter 20: Lessons from European Crisis

Always do what you set out to do.

Ray firmly believed that inaction is an enemy of progress. Each of us work for a different reason. Perhaps we are thinking about building an empire. Maybe we are hoping to improve the standard of living for our family. Or it could even be because we just want to make a big pile of money and then enjoy the rest of our lives in comfort.

Whatever the goal is, one cannot hope to reach it if one does not decide to take action to implement the ideas, goals, and plans that they had established for themselves. Many times, Ray would often talk about the fact that he can visualize where he wants to be so intensely, even when he is struggling to get there. Because of his hunger to see that visualization materialize in reality, he pushes through. He also visualizes what happens if he does not push through, and among the two choices before him, he know the direction he should be heading.

He also understands something important in life. Some people start working on their projects and realize that nothing challenging is happening to them. They get frustrated because they have heard—and probably seen or read—that challenges are a sign that they are headed in the right direction. In Ray's experience, one simply has to wait a while. The problems and challenges will present themselves. He knows that when things are calm, there is no need to look for trouble. Rather, focus on taking advantage of the relative peace and quiet to strategize and improve. Learn if you have to. Make connections or build your product even more. Perhaps you could innovate or improve. There are so many things that you can do when you have the time. When you are eventually in the thick of things, you might just wish you had used the time that you had received to do something better.

The reason Ray was successful when dealing with the European Debt Crisis was because he never stopped improving his system or learning something new. Both he and Bridgewater were constantly evolving. They learned from their mistakes, made new attempts, took risks, and went through various phases of changes.

You might have been in those situations when you were about to do something, and suddenly you were hit with a thought that went something along the lines of, "I'll start tomorrow," or "I really should try and do that."

The reality of the situation is that either one takes action or one does not. The idea of thinking or planning to do it does not have any value.

Ray also believed in connecting tasks to goals. Many people lose focus on taking actions because they are doing something that does not contribute toward their goals. To them, it might look like they are learning something or trying to improve themselves. But if those improvements and knowledge do little to affect the person's progress toward established goals, then there is no point in having them. The first thing to do is to list the goal or goals you would like to achieve. Now make a note of all the actions, activities, plans, and ideas necessary to achieve that goal. Once you have done so, work on the notes that you have made. That way, not only will you work toward achieving your goal, you are also making sure that your actions do not go to waste. Eventually, you won't lose the excitement that you had possessed when you initially visualized and imagined the end result.

Ray was about to depart his company. His main concern was finding out how to do it.

One of the many reasons why Ray was confident about his approach to the European Crisis was the fact that he would think of many situations like a case study. In fact, one of his recommendations is to imagine the problems that the case brings to the table. Now imagine the principles that apply to the case. Using this method, you will be able to apply this approach to the same scenarios when they happen in the future. After the 2008 financial crisis, Ray began to think of the entire situation like one big case study. His goal was to use certain principles to figure out the cause and effect of the crisis.

Because he had analyzed it so well, he was prepared for the European Crisis. Of course, he would always make sure that he was careful in his approach. He would ask for the feedback of numerous people and make sure that he was absolutely certain of his conclusions.

A number of successes that Ray had achieved in his lifetime were because of the company he had with him. His team at Bridgewater was greatly responsible for his personal achievements as well.

But what does it mean to create meaningful relationships? How can one create an environment where the team becomes your support?

One of the important lessons that Ray learned while growing his business was that you need to keep those people who add value to your company. To be successful, you need to surround yourself with ideas, stimuli, and even people who understand what it means to be successful.

Ray believes in the process of training. He would constantly seek ways to train his team in new methods and ideas. At the same time, he would not hold their hands. He believed in the philosophy of teaching his team how to fish rather than giving them the fish. He would then set his team free and allow them to make their own mistakes. This gave him the opportunity to improve his team, teach them valuable lessons, and discover who truly had the best interests of the company at heart. Through this method of evaluation, Ray would ensure as much as possible that he had a team that would give him support whenever he needed it and join him as he navigated difficult economic and decision-making terrains. This was certainly the case with the European Crisis as well. While Ray was definitely the one who would go on to predict the state of the economy, he could not have been completely successful if not for the team that he had at that time. From Bob Prince, who had been his partner for a long time, to Greg Jensen, the man he would consider as his godson, to many of the other members of the team. You can head over to the Bridgewater website, navigate across to the "Our Leadership" section, and then click on the Executive Bios. You will notice the faces of Bob Prince, Greg Jensen, David McCormick, and Eileen Murray. All of these members have been with him through many of the changes and challenges of Bridgewater.

# Chapter 21: Stage of Life: An End and a Beginning (2016-2017)

2016.

Sometimes, we reach a point in life when we have to bid farewell to something that has been a part of us for a long time. Sometimes, it's not the parting itself that is difficult, but how one does it that poses the biggest challenge.

Ray knew that his departure from Bridgewater would not go as smoothly as he had imagined. Now bear in mind that Ray was not the CEO of Bridgewater anymore, but he was there to guide the new management and CEOs. In other words, he was in the transition period.

It was during this period that the company would discover that they had some internal challenges to face. The investment section of Bridgewater was growing and was better than it had ever been. That was the good news. The bad news was that other areas, like recruitment and technology, were falling short of expectations. As Ray was not the CEO, he could not actively make decisions or effect changes within the company. But what he could do was provide advice and guidance to the existing CEOs. At that time, Eileen Murray and Greg Jensen were the CEOs leading Bridgewater, and even Ray could see that they were clearly stretched to their limits. When he rounded up everyone for a meeting, everyone agreed that the management of the company was not going in the direction that they had hoped. What no one could agree on was how to solve the problem. As Ray had always believed, there would always be disagreements where certain matters were concerned. It was the way he had developed the company, and it would be the way he hoped the new CEOs would also navigate the company challenges and goals. It was for this reason that no one could reach a conclusion that could help the company.

Over the next few weeks, the team would get together and discuss new strategies that they would like to implement. While there were many viewpoints and ideas, they had to slowly whittle it down to a few that they presented to their management and stakeholders committee.

In March 2016, a crucial decision was made. Greg would step down from his position as co-CEO and focus all his ideas and efforts in the position of co-Chief Investment Officer. Ray would be reinstated as the co-CEO temporarily along with Eileen Murray. But the decision was painful for both Ray and for Greg. In retrospect, Ray had realized that he had put too much responsibility on Greg by making him both the co-CIO and co-CEO. For Greg, the pain of giving up the role that he had dreamed of was truly painful. What made matters worse was the fact that the media and journalists painted a much more brutal picture of the situation than it was. They created the idea of two titans battling it out to gain the top spot. It made it seem as though Ray and Greg were on two opposing sides, each with their own views on the matter of running Bridgewater efficiently. But in the end, both Ray and Greg knew that they were making tough choices for the future of Bridgewater.

The entire situation gave Ray a little pause. How was he going to end his time at Bridgewater? What should he do before he exited the company for good? The idea that there could be another failure was something that Ray could not imagine happening. And so he sat down to decide what he would do about the situation of Bridgewater's leadership. When he began to think about what he should do, he realized that he had no idea. The whole situation concerning the CEOs was new to him, since he had been the driving force behind Bridgewater for a long time. Eventually, he reached out to a management expert named Jim Collins, who advised him to put capable CEOs on the board. But at the same time, there should be criteria that allowed the CEOs to be replaced if they were not up to the job. Ray realized that he had one more opportunity to get things right. He could not allow Bridgewater to become another sensationalist story for the journalists.

Ray began to set about company governance, which is a set of checks and balances that allows whoever is leading the organization to stay true to their course and make sure that the company continues in a manner that ensures its growth. He would never again assume that just because someone was good at one role, he or she should automatically be given another role. As he began to make difficult decisions about the company, he realized two things. The first was that David McCormack and Eileen Murray were capable CEOs who understood the vision of the company. Second, there were many other failures that the company experienced, both in terms of activities and members, that they wished they had not encountered. When dealing with the second situation, Ray knew that mistakes are lessons waiting to be learned.

With all the necessary changes being implemented, Ray ended his long tenure at Bridgewater.

As Ray mentioned, there are three phases in life. Yes, he might have ended one phase of life.

But it was the beginning of the third.

# Chapter 22: Lessons from End and Beginning

Decision-making is not such a simple act to undertake. In many cases, there are sacrifices to be made and hard choices to go through.

Ray had spent his entire life making the tough calls. But more than simply making them, he had also been studying them to understand their mechanics. He had been applying various systems and rules to attain what he wanted the most and reduced the risks that he might have to eventually face.

What he came to realize is that when people make decisions, their thought processes are mainly subconscious. This is a remarkable thing to realize on your own, but it does come when someone has experience making decisions. In fact, it is psychologically proven that our decisions are mainly subconscious. Let us try to understand this point by using an example.

Imagine that you are heading home from work or any other place. You know the route so well that you could probably head home blindfolded. It doesn't matter if you are driving or walking; the point is that you know how to reach your destination without thinking too much about it. On the way, you realize that today you are going to prepare a rather special dinner. Tomorrow is the start of the weekend, after all! Thoughts about the weekend lull you into deep imaginations of what you would do about it. Should you invite your friends over or should you go visit your parents? As you think about your friends, you recollect the time you had all gone swimming at that incredible lake just outside the city. Speaking of which, weren't you thinking of leaving the city for a vacation? Perhaps Bali sounds nice at this time of the year. Wait a minute, wasn't Bali recently in the news for—

Hold on.

You have just arrived at your destination. But it's odd. You don't remember most of the journey. It almost seems as though your conscious brain took a short nap while you were heading home.

The reality is that our subjective experience is divided into two forms: conscious and subconscious. We would always like to believe that our conscious mind is the more powerful one among the two, but research has shown otherwise. The example above illustrates just how powerful your subconscious mind is because while you were consciously thinking about something, your subconscious mind was taking care of everything else, including guiding you toward home. In fact, think about where you are right now. You are reading the words on this page. Of course, you are using your conscious mind to focus on the words and derive meaning from them. But what is controlling the rest of your body? What is managing your rate of breathing, the blinking of your eyes, the way you are holding the book or sitting down to read on a device, the fact that your lips are not drooping, and your body temperature and other calculations to keep you functioning as you continue reading?

The answer is that it all comes down to your subconscious. One of the important connections about the subconscious mind is that it is largely emotional. And it is here that we come to see its influence in our everyday life. You see, according to neuroscience, our decisions are largely emotional. This means that the subconscious has a bigger impact on our decision-making process than we realize.

Ray understood this basic fact. It was why he always insisted on never making a decision based on emotions and was of the firm belief that one should always take logical steps before arriving at a particular conclusion.

When it came to decision-making, he believed that one should create a systematic approach to making those decisions. It should be done in such a manner that they can describe the process to someone else easily and even teach others to follow the steps taken.

But is there a way to develop good decision-making skills? Can someone learn to decide things better?

There is.

### *Step 1: Learn about the harmful emotions that affect your decision-making process*

Do you get frustrated too easily? Are you unable to control your temper? Do certain sad memories plague you while you are thinking about your decisions? Ray believes that before you make any decision, allow yourself to take a step back and evaluate everything with a critical eye. Think about where you are drawing your knowledge from. Check to see if you have all the facts and information necessary to give you as much awareness about the situation as possible. Think about where you are drawing your knowledge from. Are you certain that you are getting an accurate picture? Can you trust the source?

### *Step 2: Don't keep your views biased*

Many people have troubling bottling up their emotions and end up taking a biased view on things. For example, people usually end up having confirmation bias, which is a psychological phenomenon where they only look at the information they believe in and refuse to consider any information that is opposing or against their thought process. If you find yourself in such a position, do not think about drawing any conclusions, creating ideas, or establishing goals. Simply choose to step away from the problem for a while.

### *Step 3: Analyze the situation*

Next, analyze the situation at hand and create as many solutions as you can. There are not many situations when you can use the first thought that comes into your mind as the solution to the problem, and it immediately turns out to be right. Prepare a list of solutions. It does not matter if you feel that some of them are absurd. The idea is to cover all areas as possible. Once the solutions are listed, you can then use the process of elimination to bring down the list of possible solutions. Eventually, you are going to have a few solutions that might all sound plausible in theory. At this point, you simply have to use logic and information to think about which of the remaining solutions is ideal for you.

Test out your beliefs with people. Let them argue against the points that you have established. Allow them to find loopholes and disadvantages in your line of reasoning. But make sure that you are not listening to everything they say blindly. Take in all the information they provide and think about them. Some of the arguments and theories against your decision or idea might have some weight. But the way to find them out is by once again using logic and information.

Finally, you will be able to discover a solution that best fits your scenario.

This was the same course of action that Ray took when he was appointing the new CEO. He understood that he could not make the decision on his own. So he took the help of a management expert to give him some tips. He analyzed the feedback and then carefully put together a plan of action.

Ray also liked to believe that one should not just think about the conclusions that people make, but also the reasoning behind them. That is because sometimes you might hear a suggestion and actually think that it could not be viable for your situation or that it sounds too simple. But often, an explanation might convince you why the conclusion drawn is actually something you should think about more. Never shrug off advice provided by people who are experienced. If they apply to your case, then why not use them?

# Chapter 23: Stage of Life: Third Act (2017-Now)

Looking back, Ray realized that that over the course of his life, his perspective had changed numerous times.

When he was starting out and learning his way around the markets, everything looked intimidating. Things were challenging and terrifying. Whenever he was faced with a problem, he would feel like any mistake he made would be his last.

What he realized through those times is that the unknown is always terrifying. When we begin to face problems in the beginning, they always take us off guard because they are issues that we have never faced before.

Back during the days of the caveman, humans had a natural fear of the unknown. This was a sort of defense mechanism. It allowed us to keep away from strange places, prevent us from venturing out too far from the group where there was relative safety, or try and take unnecessary risks. As time went on, this evolutionary habit persisted. It does not mean that we never needed such reactions and thoughts. No matter what age of human history we belonged to, we were always cautious, and that saved us from making rash decisions and taking uncalculated risks. Fast forward to the present, and we still have the same fears within us. We know that the unknown features challenges that we might not be ready for. That is why they are called the unknown. But the biggest risk one takes is not facing the unknown; it is avoiding taking risk at all in the first place.

To Ray, taking risks was something that had become part of his life since a young age. He was always looking for new challenges and new ideas to experiment with. This is what allowed him to face the challenges later on. No matter how intimidating it became.

But while pondering the challenges in his life, Ray began to think about the challenges that other people faced. More importantly, he thought about those people who did not have the same opportunities that the rest of the world was provided. Ray turned his attention to philanthropy.

Ray's first experience with philanthropy would not exactly be termed as such. It was the 1990s, the time when Bridgewater was steadily growing and Ray was in the process of creating the many principles that would guide his company. At that time, Matt, his eldest son, was turning 16 and was fairly fluent in Mandarin. During one of the family visits that Ray used to arrange, Matt began to visit a Chinese orphanage. While talking to the staff at the orphanage, Matt would make a remarkable discovery:

with just $500, he could radically save people's lives. Seeing that his son was serious about playing his part in helping the people of the orphanage, Ray gave him $500. Once Matt saw that he could indeed make a difference in people's lives, he wanted to do more.

At that time, Ray's friend, Paul Tudor Jones, who was also starting up his own investment management company, decided to provide some tips to Matt and give him vital information. Most importantly, he taught Matt how he could create a 501(c)(3) foundation.

A 501(c)(3) foundation is a type of nonprofit organization that has been labeled as a tax-exempt, charitable organization by the Internal Revenue Service. The "charity" has a broad classification by the IRS. Typically, it means any organization or entity that has been established for the purpose of providing educational, religious, literary, scientific, charitable, public safety, developing programs for national or international sports, or preventing cruelty to animals and children. Under such conditions, a 501(c)(3) foundation can either be a private foundation or public charity.

501(c)(3) foundations become classified as public charities when they are any of the below:

- The organizations are hospitals, churches, or medical research facilities that are attached to various schools, colleges, hospitals, universities, and hospitals.

- Establish and schedule active fundraising programs, while at the same time receiving contributions from various sources, whether those sources are public or private.

- Receive income through activities that are part of the organization's goals and aims.

- Provide support to any other charitable institution or set-up.

If they are not part of the list above, then they are usually classified as private foundations.

Matt was left with a choice. He could create a public foundation, but that would mean that he would have to be actively part of that organization. At that time, Matt wasn't thinking of becoming a philanthropist in a full-time capacity. For that reason, he created a private foundation in 2000 and named it the China Care Foundation. He was still in high school.

Not only would Matt do as much work as possible for the foundation, but he would also bring his family to the orphanages to introduce them to the special-needs children. Ray and his family would not only be moved to do something for them, but would come to love them as well. At that time, Matt would also begin to struggle with difficult decisions. Since they would not have enough money to help out all the children, Matt would sometimes be in the tough position of deciding which children would live and which would not receive adequate medical treatment. But watching his son overcome those difficulties, strengthen his mental resolve, and continue to make a difference would inspire Ray as well. Often Matt would sacrifice a big night out in the city with his friends just so he could save extra money for the orphanage. Ray began to realize that with the progress Bridgewater was making, it was time for him to make a change in the world. In 2003, Ray set up an organization with his family. He wanted the work that goes into the philanthropic endeavor to be something that he would do with his family.

Ray realized something else at that time. Coming up with a solution to give away money is as challenging as making it. There are many steps that needs to be established and much research done to make sure that the money goes where it is intended. More importantly, Ray realized that he would have to start making careful decisions about the money he was giving away. He needed to know how much money he would have to save for his family, how much he needed to give to close relatives, and just how much he would have to put into a charitable organization. The main reason for so much thought was that, eventually, he wanted to leave behind enough money for his sons so that they would not worry about education, healthcare, and the initial boost required to start their careers. All of this occurred before Bridgewater was the success that it was, and so Ray did not have all the financial resources that he now has to make decisions easily.

Additionally, as Ray started taking care of multiple causes, he realized how fast he would lose money. While his main concern was the foundation and the help he was providing, he began to notice that even though the money would be spent quickly, it would be too thinly distributed among the various causes and not make any difference in any of them. He would have to make another tough decision. Ray consulted with other people and discovered that no matter how rich they were, they faced the same problem as well. It would be challenging to manage the flow of cash when there were many requirements for each cause.

At the same time, Ray was also thinking about which charities he should focus on. His wife Barbara was passionate about helping children who did not have access to proper school systems in the state of Connecticut to receive a proper education. She had discovered that nearly 22% of children in that state would fall into two categories: disengaged or disconnected. This meant that either the education system wouldn't be able to do much for them, or that they would not have any connection to a proper education. During one of her studies, she discovered that nearly 10,000 children did not have winter coats. With help from Ray, she sent in the required donation to make sure that the children received their coats.

Ray always thought that he was part of the "land of opportunity," but after seeing the conditions of many people around him, he realized that some of the struggles are much closer to home. He was also of the opinion that everyone deserves to have equal opportunities and that it is the fundamental right of everyone to have access to education. Without that, he understood the fact that those children might eventually grow up to be adults who won't be able to contribute valuably to society. In turn, those members of society might resort to lives of crime, which might increase the number of people incarcerated. This eventually becomes expensive for the country as a whole. How expensive? According to Vera Institute of Justice, the cost of managing jails across the country had grown to $22.2 billion. This was in the year 2011. It was around $5.7 billion in the year 1983. All of these facts told Ray something, and he wanted to get to the root of the problem.

At the same time, Ray was also connected with nature. He wanted to make a positive change to the oceans of the world. More importantly, he wanted to contribute to those environmentalists and scientists who sought a solution to the problem of plastic polluting various water bodies of the world.

The more organized Ray's charitable foundations became, the more he could make a real difference in the world. And long after he left the company, he and his family were focused on continuing to make a difference.

While he was making a difference to the world, he often wondered about the difference he would be making to his family as well. He had already established a trust in their name that would allow them to share in the wealth should something happen to him, and he would be long gone from this world. It was not just the idea that his family should have more than enough to take care of themselves and their families in turn, but that they should be able to set up any venture that they intended to without worrying about the financial resources available to them. At the same time, he also wanted to leave his children the gift of knowledge.

Ray began to think about his life and the experiences he had gone through. From the biggest challenges to the most painful situations. He began to view them in a different light; one that brought with it lessons and important knowledge. Instead of allowing them to frustrate or overwhelm him, he looked at it as life's way of letting him know that there was something to learn. In fact, he realized that he had dealt with the pains and losses in his life like he had most of his challenges; as a puzzle to be solved or a game to be played.

He also thought back to his influences, especially those who had also gone on to build successful empires and organizations. One of his greatest inspirations was Steve Jobs. When he learned more about Jobs' life, he realized that it was filled with its own set of pains, challenges, and disappointments.

And all of these lessons—from his pains and struggles to his inspirations—were all something that he wanted to give to his children. He began to put more effort into the book that he was writing, titled *Principles: Life and Work*.

However, while he was writing the book, another thought struck him. He was already making sure that he was contributing through his charity. Now, he was providing his children the gift of all the wealth of experience that he had. What if he could combine the two? But how could he do it? He needed to connect with people. Sure, they could buy the book and then use that to gain knowledge. But what if there was a way to connect with them instantly and then provide the knowledge that he had?

Ray realized that he knew of one powerful tool that could help him connect to millions of people around the world: social media.

With that thought in mind, Ray began to be actively present in various social media networks, imparting the knowledge that he had shared in *Principles: Life and Work* and connecting with as many people as possible. He even opened his own Reddit account where he has a specific section that he personally handles. There, people can ask him questions about life, his work, the principles that he follows, and anything else where they could seek out his advice and feedback on a number of topics. He also released an app titled "Principles in Action" that allowed users to discover more of his principles through the popularity of an app.

In the end, he was able to achieve his mission of providing more knowledge to the world, leaving behind a legacy for his family, and setting up various charitable institutions.

# Chapter 24: Lessons from Third Act

Steve Jobs had once talked about how work might end up filling a large part of our lives. He talked about how the best way to actually be satisfied with what we do is to focus on doing great work.

But what exactly is great work? How did Ray Dalio know that the work he did was great? What motivated him to continue forward?

Growing up, Ray would never focus on something that he did not like. In fact, he was mostly forgetful about many things simply because he found them uninteresting or they were not valuable to him. There is an important lesson there.

In our quest to find greatness or discover things that we would like to do, we often forget to refer to the people who know best—us. In one of the Reddit posts, a user asked Ray what he would do if he was 18 years old in the year 2019. How would he approach his life and how he would start his career? Ray responded by saying that one should choose to follow their passion, but at the same time, they should think about the practicalities of following it. He went on to also talk about gaining some real- world experience to gain different perspectives about what someone would like to do.

Essentially, what Ray was trying to say was that having a passion is good. But it is equally important to think about whether one can use it to become successful in life. Let's take an example to highlight this. Let us assume that someone has a passion to paint. While it is important to follow that passion, one must also think if taking that course of action would help establish themselves as a successful individual in the future. Can they make something out of their passion? Do they have enough options to explore that passion? If they are not certain about the path they are taking, then how can they use that passion and turn it into an instrument of success? For example, since the person has a passion for painting, can they use that in another medium? How about graphic design? That way, not only will they be able to exercise their creative and artistic side, but also be able to enhance it through various means. Or they could become artists for book covers or comics, where they can eventually find publishers to check out their work and use their skills for authors, writers, and storytellers. When we logic to think about the decisions we are about to make and the actions that we would like to take, we can direct our life toward meaningful and wonderful goals.

But why should someone aim for such meaning and sense of accomplishment? Isn't it enough to simply earn a salary and be able to afford things?

This comes down to Ray's three phases of life theory, where he thinks that in phase one we are dependent on people. In phase two, people are dependent on us and, finally, in phase three, we are completely independent to do the things that we would like to do. After going through numerous challenges and reaching the point that he has reached, Ray knows that we should all strive to enter phase three. We need to reach a point where we are free to do many things that we did not have the pleasure of doing when we were struggling to reach our goals.

After 2017, Ray focused on his charitable foundations and leaving behind a legacy for his children. He wanted to give back to the world and to his family. Eventually, that is a goal that everyone should aim to reach.

However, there is another piece of advice that Ray gave to people on his Reddit board. One user asked Ray about passion and if there is any amount of 'grind' involved in the work. Ray responded by saying that often, it is like climbing Mount Everest. There are people who enjoy doing it. They gain some thrill from knowing that they have conquered the highest peak in the world. But to reach to the top, one has to do the climbing as well, and the climb is not going to be easy. Life is similar. It is good to follow your passion. But the two key points to remember are that one has to have a realistic approach to their passion and that eventually, you will still have to work hard to reach a certain point. Regardless of what you do, there is never a point where things will go smoothly and in your favor.

Then what about the work itself? Won't everything become simply about the "grind"?

Ray has an answer for this as well. In fact, another Reddit user asked him what advice he would give to someone who is in their teenage years. He responded by saying that they should find something that excites them (in other words, their passion) and make sure to have fun while they are doing what they like.

When you find something that gives your life meaning, you realize that no matter how challenging things get, how much hard work you have to put into the task, or how many disappointments you feel along the way, you will eventually come to enjoy the whole process. Sure, the pain and challenges are not exactly what one would call "fun," but they are only going to be intimidating for that particular moment. Remember how Ray explained that things only seem big when you look at them closely? The same is true for many situations in life. When we face something, it usually tends to look menacing and intimidating. We have come face-to-face with an unknown challenge, and it frightens us. We begin to wonder if we make a mistake, will it be the end of our journey? Will we have to give up all our dreams and settle back into something more mediocre? The most important thing to do is to never give up at that moment. Eventually, at a later time in your life, you might end up looking back and thinking to yourself, "Why was I ever worried about that?"

But one's desire to do something never ends, as it became evident with Ray. He found a new purpose. He was focused on his own struggles during the course of his work. Once he stepped away from the company, he began to focus on the struggles of others.

That would be another important lesson to learn from him. We should try and aim to give back to the world, even in small ways. You can pick any cause that matters to you. It could be for animal welfare. You could decide to help the children of the world. You can make a difference to the environment. Whatever change you would like to see in this world, you can contribute toward that change in a small way. Some people are of the opinion that their contribution is too small to matter. That in the grand scheme of things, they would have hardly made any effort at all. In reality, it is never about how big or small the difference you have made is; it is about whether you have made a difference at all.

# **Conclusion**

Ray has reached the part of his life where he wants to focus on helping others become successful. That is because he has attained enough success that he is not particularly seeking more of it.

Through the many events in his life, Ray has been constantly learning. Some lessons were readily available to him while others were learned through some rather painful and difficult situations. Eventually, he compiled all of his learnings and lessons in one book that he wanted to share with the world.

One of the most frequent lessons that he likes to impart on people is the idea of humility. He had learned the hard way what it would cost if one approached a situation or opportunity with arrogance. Looking through his Reddit, you might come across one comment where the user mentions how he or she saw Ray in an interview where the interviewer was obviously trying to be crass to generate some sort of sensationalist reaction from Ray. Throughout the interview, Ray maintained a sense of calm professionalism. The user respected that of Ray and wanted to know how he could learn to do that. Ray explained that in life, you need to have a sense of balance. You need to be able to look at things objectively instead of reacting to them emotionally. When you look at life in such a manner, you begin to evaluate everything calmly and with logical reasoning. At the same time, one should also have strong principles that they uphold. These principles can be anything. The one criteria that they should follow is that they should reflect the true nature of the person holding the principles. For example, if you believe that life is short and you must live it to the fullest, it is a principle that you should have formed after careful consideration of your goals, your ambitions, and how you measure success. It should not be because you happened to read a very attractive message on your social media feed that talks about living your life to the fullest. This does not mean that you cannot take inspiration from other sources. The process of learning can happen from various sources. However, when you eventually choose a set principles or even believe in something, you should do so based on your values and character.

Ray also believes in the power of failure. He understands that it is important to fail well. Because when someone fails, they understand the pain and discomfort that comes along with those failures. Most importantly, they learn valuable lessons that they can use to not just prevent those failures from happening again, but to drive their life in a better direction.

Through all the lessons that Ray is trying to teach, he wants people to look at his life and learn to keep their goals in mind, reflect on them, and never give up on achieving them. If you go through his social media profiles, you will see a man who is living up to the promise he made to educate and help people find their way. Look through his Twitter profile and you will see a list of helpful tips, useful advice, and insights into the world of business and personal life.

•

Ray is a dreamer. He believes in the power of trying to visualize where you would like to be in your life. In one of his tweets, he mentions that he likes making dreams happen. He also thinks that in life, there is nothing better than working on those dreams and transforming them into reality. The key word in that equation is reality. How are the dreams connected to reality? What principles and rules have you established to make sure that what you are doing has a realistic approach? Because in the end, how you approach your dreams decides what kind of dreamer you are. You can be an idle dreamer; a person who is so lost in the world of his or her dreams that no action has been taken to inch closer toward making them happen. Or you can be a doer; someone who believes that actions define the course of his or her life.

Ray's life is an insight on how you can face your struggles, and how you can evolve not just as a person, but as a manager and eventually, a leader.

He admires Steve Jobs and believes that there is so much one can learn from him. But you only have to see the presence he has in people's lives to know that Ray himself has made a mark of his own. His life does not merely teach lessons that encourage focusing on your dreams and to keep fighting until you get there. He also shows us how to manage a team, how life is about maintaining those precious relationships, about the pain of failure and why it is important, about leadership and sacrifice, and even about being charitable. One of his inspirations was the late and first Prime Minister of Singapore. He was famously known for saying that the task of leaders is centered on establishing a strong framework that allows them to learn, work to the best of their capabilities, work productively, and be able to reward well. If that is indeed the case, then Ray has done all of that successfully, and through many tough lessons in life.

One that inspires people. One that compels people to achieve their dreams.

If we were to examine all the lessons that Ray could teach us, there are plenty to squeeze into just one book. It is for this reason that he is splitting his ideas and thoughts into two different books: one that focuses on life and work, with the other focusing on investments and economics. But there is one thing that we have understood quite clearly and that might not require multiple books. If there was a pantheon of people who have gone on to make it big (his net worth is a little over $16 billion) while starting small, then Ray Dalio would be in it. His life is not just a story that could probably make it into an HBO mini-series, but one that is capable of inspiring many.

Ray feels that he has done his best to pass along the messages and principles of his life on to others. With the number of people who interact with him on his social profiles, it seems that he has indeed done it.

# References

Beevor, A. (2013). *The Second World War*. Back Bay Books.

Blinder, A. (2013). After the Music Stopped: The Financial Crisis, the Response, and the Work Ahead. Penguin Books.

Dalio, R. (2017). *Principles*. Simon & Schuster.

Homberger, E., & Hudson, A. (2005). The Historical Atlas of New York City: A Visual Celebration of 400 Years of New York City's History. New York: H. Holt and Co.

Kahneman, D. (2011). *Thinking, Fast and Slow*. New York: Farrar, Straus & Giroux Inc.

Lapavitsas, C., & Kouvélakis, E. (2012). *Crisis in the Eurozone*. London: Verso.

Lee, K. (1998). The Singapore Story: Memoirs of Lee Kuan Yew. Singapore: Prentice Hall.

Printed in Poland
by Amazon Fulfillment
Poland Sp. z o.o., Wrocław